WATER BATH CANNING & PRESERVING COOKBOOK FOR BEGINNERS

The Complete Beginner's Guide with 300+ Tasty Recipes to Water Bath and Pressure Canning for Vegetables, Meats, Meals in a Jar, and Plenty's of Additional Foodstuffs

SOPHIE HUMBLE

Table of Contents

CHAPTER 9:   STRAWBERRY FREEZE JAM98

CHAPTER 10:   FERMENTED RECIPES......100

Introduction

What is Canning?

To make the meaning and definition of canning simple and short to the point, canning can be described as a direction of packaging meats, poultry, fish, vegetables, and fruits in glass jars and then heating the jar to kill any active bacteria or enzymes. To build on the canning definition, there are two types of canning techniques, which are Water bath Canning and Pressure Canning.

Raw Packing (Cold Packing) vs. Hot Packing

When you fill the jars with foods that have not been heated or cooked or food that you have no intentions of cooking after you take it out of the jar is called raw packing, which is normally used for and fruit and vegetables.

Hot packing refers to boiled or cooked food, and this is normally used for jam, jelly, pie filling, tomato sauce, soups and broths, stews, and poultry. Hot packing is great for removing the additional air bubbles and maintaining the natural color of the food items.

Benefits of canning

By canning, the shelf life of products can be increased significantly, and food remains edible for much longer than it ordinarily would.

Studies have found that canned foods are not lacking in the nutritional value that fresh foods have and sometimes even serve as healthier alternatives.

The general discussion for this book will be about canning and preserving food only using jars, there are other ways to process canned foods other than jars, but that won't be discussed in this book. Just in case you are a beginner or some who needs a refresher in the course of the canning, I want to start off by giving you the definition of canning and the added benefits that go along with it once you are committed to adding it to your repertoire of cooking and using it to save and preserve your food.

The purpose of this book is to give you a greater knowledge of the concept of canning and what it will entail. The main methods of canning will be discussed, and you will be given pointers on the methods to try out first, as a beginner, and the methods you should try out when you have become more advanced as a canner.

You will find that as you follow the instructions provided by this book, you will become more comfortable about your skills as a canner – even if you have never done it before. This book will also include a number of exciting recipes that you will be able to try out at home. The recipes will only serve as a guide for you; we have left you with room to add your own touch to your foods.

You will find delicious recipes in this book that demonstrate each of the different food preservation techniques. There's something here for novices and experienced food preservationists alike. Through this book, you will understand the components of the recipes that are responsible for safely preserving food. Is it the acidity of the vinegar, the hotter-than-boiling-water heat of pressure canning, or some other factor? With this book in hand, you won't have to guess.

Chapter 1: Canning Times

People have been preserving food since the beginning of time. This Direction of preservation originated in France in the 19th century. The French government was looking for a way to make food readily available to the troops year-round so that their military operations were not affected. Nicolas Appert devised a Direction of canning that laid the steppingstones for what is performed today.

Canning made its advent into America in 1812, when Robert Ayars set up the first canning factory in New York City.

In the 21st century, food preservation is more than a way to stock up for the winter, save on the grocery bill, or make some cute food gifts for the holidays. Although it can certainly be all of those things, contemporary food preservation is also a way to reduce your carbon footprint by having locally grown or raised foods on hand year-round.

Statistics show that one in four households in the United States do home canning for their own personal use. In fact, the rising number of people who have seen the benefits of eating locally is also the reason why home canning is being revived in many households in the country. This chapter will deal with the technical side of home canning.

Preparing preserves, jams and jellies at home have become an exciting hobby for millions of people. Also, it is a great way to save bucks and feel independent to make them whenever you need and whenever your mood strikes. Commercially available preserves, jams, relishes, etc. are not only costly as compared to homemade versions, but they are also added with preservatives, additives, artificial colors, and chemicals.

One great advantage of homemade canning is that you can prepare it from fresh ingredients and can ensure that what you are consuming is totally free of additives and preservatives. Another great advantage is that you can keep total control over ingredients quantities; not everyone likes the same amount of sweetness or sourness in preserves and jams. This way, you can adjust sugar quantity as well as savory ingredients such as vinegar, lemon juice, etc. to suit your taste.

Homemade canning gives you another advantage of preparing them in small quantities; when you prepare them in small quantities, these canning recipes maintain their natural flavours. It takes less space to store and you get to enjoy fresh batches by preparing them at shorter intervals. Short batches provide you with the freedom to make different varieties every time and rotating them as per seasonal ingredients. And if it gets spoiled due to external environmental issues, the wastage amount is quite less.

FOOD PRESERVATION

Dehydrating

Dehydrating with a food dehydrator is the best method these days. You have control over temperature, time, and air flow. You place food on a tray, close the lid, and heat at the appropriate temperature with an electrical heating element for the given time. Times vary depending on what you're drying and how much. A fan circulates heat around the food, while vents allow the moist air to escape.

Although there are many methods to dehydrate food such as sun drying and oven drying, the most convenient method is by using an electric dehydrator. Why? Because it is an easy and hassle-free way to dehydrate your food.

You can get commercial electrical dehydrators from the market that matches your needs, or you can go for DIY dehydrator at home.

DIY home dehydrator

You can construct your dehydrator, if you need to produce large batches of dried foods, from a wooden framed box. All you need is constant heat (gas burner) and airflow (a fan) and few shelves or trays to put food on. However, it becomes difficult to control the temperature levels if you are a beginner, and sometimes it results in a complete mess due to a complicated cleaning process. You need a lot of experimentation and testing to achieve the optimum temperature levels in DIY dehydrators.

Electric dehydrators

If you plan to dry your food regularly, then investing in a commercial electrical dehydrator is the best option. They can handle large quantities of food, and the best part is, you can control the temperature and air circulation without putting much effort. In a useful and well-made electric dehydrator, the temperature remains constant throughout the drying process with the help of a thermostatically controlled heating system, and proper airflow is achieved through a built-in fan to ensure complete evaporation.

You can get a small unit with 4 or 5 trays under a hundred dollars if you want to dry small batches in one go. However, if you intend to dry a lot of food at once, you can get a commercial dehydrator with ten trays or more.

The Freezing Method

You probably know that many people jumped on the wagon when it comes to preserving their food. What if I told you that even if you've never tried Canning alone, is there an approach that anyone can learn easily? Home preserves-the freezing process is the best way to start.

Although there are many ways to store and store food available to try the freezing method is a favorite among Canning enthusiasts for a number of reasons:

The freezing approach takes less time than other home canning methods.

Learning the process of freezing fresh fruits and vegetables is easy and accessible even for beginners.

Generally, the cost involved in freezing your food is minimal.

Frozen Fruits and vegetables can be stored for a year without affecting the taste and quality of food.

You have the will to prepare meals quickly by simply opening the freezer.

Almost all vegetables require sunburn before freezing. Bleaching is a step in the process of preparing food for freezing. This is not difficult to learn, but there are defined processing times for vegetables to blanch based on which ones you want to freeze. There are some exceptions to this rule, such as onions and fresh green peppers that do not require sunburn to store them in the freezer.

Fruits are another source that does not need to be blanched before freezing. Typically, the fruits should be peeled (animated even if necessary) and have a preservative applied to them such as fresh fruit or lemon juice to discourage any discoloration and to block the fresh taste of the fruit that will freeze.

Now you know that the House preserves - the method of freezing is an easy way even for a beginner to get started. There are steps to this process, but they are not difficult to learn. You can also do it.

Chapter 2: Water Bath Canning

The process of Water bath canning is when you boil your food in water for a specific amount of time. This process of water canning is what you would want to use for high acidic foods. The determining factor of what can be considered to be acid food, are those that have the pH of 4.6 or lower. Basically, your main acidic foods that you would probably use the Waterbath Canning Direction for would be lemons, tomatoes, fruits, pickles, relishes, vinegar and some condiments.

The reason why you can use water canning Direction with acid food is because the acid is so strong in the food that it blocks and destroys the growth of bacteria, when boiled to a certain temperature.

Water Bath Canning

For water bath canning, you're basically placing your food in a jar, wiping down the rims, affixing the lid to the jar, boiling the jars, and then removing them when it's safe. Here are more detailed Directions: for this canning Direction:

First, make sure your jars, lids, and bands work before you use them. Don't use jars that are chipped, scratched, or compromised in any way. You don't want them to break during the canning process. Wash your jars, lids, and bands in warm water with soap, and dry them. You don't have to do any excessive sterilization. If they are clean, you will be fine.

Heat the jars in hot water while you prepare the food. It should not be boiling water, and you don't have to cover the jars. Simply let them rest in a pot that's half-ful with hot water. This will prevent the jars from breaking when you put hot food inside them.

Prepare your recipe with whatever foods you plan to can. Remove the hot jar from the water, using a jar lifter. Fill the jars with your food, using a large spoon or a funnel. Leave at least 1/2 an inch of space at the top of the jar. Remove any air bubbles by pressing down on the food with a spatula or spoon.

Remove any food from the rim of the jar by wiping clean with a damp cloth. Apply the band and the lid until it is tight.

Place the jars in a large pot of water, allowing the water to cover the jars completely. Heat the water until it boils. Processing time will depend on your recipe.

When it's done, remove the jars and allow them to sit at room temperature. You'll want to leave them undisturbed for at least 12 hours.

You can find these prepping tools at Amazon, Targets, and any hardware and local grocery store. You might even already possess most of these items in your arsenal of cooking ware. Once you make these purchases you will most likely never have to buy them again. Please make sure read and follow this section carefully to avoid any unnecessary mistakes that could potentially be dangerous.

Water bath Canners

The water bath canner is a very large pot that normally has capacity size of 20 (or larger) quarts. It comes with a lid that seals tight in order to keep the pressure and the temperature high within the can. This canner also comes equipped with a wooden or wire rack.

The purpose of the rack is to keep the boiling water equally distributed around the jars in order to make sure that all of the jars get processed. The rack allows for the jars to have their own space within the pot, meaning you don't have to worry about your jars touching each other which could lead to breakage within the pot.

Don't Want to Buy a Water Canner

Now let's say that you are not interested into buying a fancy water canner or you already have a pretty large pot, than instead of buying a water canner you can save yourself some money and just use what you have, or just buy a large pot.

In order to skip buying a water canner you will need any type of large metal pot that will be deep enough to put jars into the pan while also allowing there to be at least an inch of boiling water over the top of it. Now there is such thing of having a pot that is too large. The standard pot for canning should not be four inches wider than your stove burner. If your pot is too large than certain jars will not get process as equally as the others.

Next step is replacing the rack; you still need something to acts as a buffer to keep the jars from bumping into each other and cracking inside the pot. You can use a clean dish towel to wrap and the jars or you could also place rings inside of the pot to hold the jars in place.

Pressure Canners

For review purpose you only use the pressure canning Direction for low acid foods such as your meats, poultry, fish, and vegetables.

A pressure canner is a large pot but the difference between this canner and the water canner is that the pressure canner is a stainless steel heavy duty pot that is made strong enough to endure extreme steam and pressure. The lid of this canner comes with a vent and also a rubber seal to stop any air from seeping into the can and disrupting the process. A rack is also included with the pressure canner and serves the same purpose as the rack in the water canner.

One more thing to make note of is that there are two types of pressure canners. There is one pressure that comes with a dial and there is another that comes with a weighted a gauge. In my opinion one is not better than the other and they both provide the same end result.

Jars

There are three parts to a jar; the metal screw band, metal lid, and the jar. The jar is where you will put the food that you want to process. Some of the types of jars that can be used to canned food items include Mason jar and Ball jars. You could also use any type of jar that is threaded and comes with a self-sealing lids. Also, these jars have to have a wide opening approximately about three inches, so that you are able easily empty and fill it.

Jars can come in many sizes ranging from 1/2 a pint all the way up to 1/2 gallon. The can be reused numerous times until they wear out. You will know that a jar is worn out if it has any type of chip or fraction within the glass. If the jar is even slightly chipped than it will disrupt the seal and possibly break in the canner while you are in the process of canning your food.

Jar Lids

The lid is one of the most important parts when it comes to sealing the jar and keeping out the air. The jars that are sold in today's market come with a two piece lid that has a selfsealing compound that is basically a metal disc and a ring.

Since the lid is small and thin and is easily softened when it is heated, it is a must that you dispose of the lid once you are done using it. But you metal screw bands/rings can be reuse numerous times because it's only job is to hold the lid in place while it's being processed.

Other Utensils to Use

Here is a quick reference to other utensils that you will use during your canning process.

Jar lifter/ Tongs: Needed to lift the hot jars out of the boiling hot water.

Funnel: For pouring the food into the jars. And minimizes the mess.

Lid wand: It magnetically allows you to place the lid on or off the the can.

Clean cloths: Necessary for cleaning the rim of the jars and other messes.

Narrow, flat rubber spatula: Used to remove the air bubbles.

Equipment Not To Use for Canning

- Pressure Cooker
- Dishwashers
- Microwave ovens

- Fruit Jars
- Mayonnaise Jars
- Metal Spatula

Preparing the Jars for Canning

It is necessary that you always use a clean sterilized jar before you begin the process of canning. When you a clean a jar you ensure that the food that is being canned will have a long shelflife, while also removing and destroying any bacteria, yeast, or fungi that might be in the glass jar. The Direction of sterilizing the jars is quick and easy should never be skipped over.

Jar Cleaning and Preparation

The first thing you want to do to the jar glass, which is not heated, is simply wash it with dish detergent using hot water. You have the options of either washing it by hand or using the dishwasher, either or works just fine. You want to make sure that you rinse out the dish detergent thoroughly, because any leftover residue might cause your food items to turn a different color or might affect the taste of it.

Let it be noted that this is a preheating Direction to sterilizing the jars, and does not actually sterilize the glass jars.

Sterilizing the Empty Glass Jars

The sterilizing procedure takes around thirty minutes and difficulty level is easy. There are three Directions that you can use to sterilize your jars, and each Direction will be discussed in the upcoming sections. This is a necessary part of the canning and it should not be skipped.

The Oven

The oven sterilizing Direction is probably the most used technique. Wrap the two shelves in your oven with two layers of newspaper. Make sure there is enough room for the jars around the head space level, so that glass jar is not touching the top of the oven and the same goes for the bottom part of the oven.

Heat the oven to a maximum heat level to 275 degrees. If you try to make the oven any hotter than the suggest temperature, you will risk the jars breaking in the oven. Put the clean glass jars inside the oven on the shelves. Make sure that the jars have their own space and are not touching each other.

Leave the jars in the oven for twenty to thirty minutes. To remove the jars from the oven you want use very thick oven mitts and take the jars out and place them on a cutting board.

Dishwater Direction

You can use this technique only if you have dishwater that has the capabilities of reaching a high temperature. Place the clean jars inside of the dishwasher giving enough adequate space where the glasses are not touching each other.

You want to run the dishwasher for as long as it takes you to get your food ready. For instance if you are canning green beans then you want to boil the green beans at a high temperature (hot packing), and until your green beans are done you don't want to take the jars out the dishwater , because your jars will cool down before you get the chance of filling it with the prepped green beans.

Microwave Direction

I know that I stated never to use the microwave in the actual canning process but you can use it to sterilize a jar. This technique is best used if you are only preparing one jar and need a quick way to sterilize your jar. To use this Direction you want to put the clean jars in the microwave, but you want the jars to be a little wet.

Microwave the jars on a high setting for 3045 seconds. I would only use this Direction for one jar because you want to make sure that the heat is distributed equally. Another key note is to make sure that your timing is together with whatever food you plan on canning, especially if you are hot packing.

Sterilization Reminders and Other Mentions

Try to go beyond and above when you are sterilizing the jars, such as repeating the preheat cleaning Direction several times before you actually begin to sterilize the jars with heat.

Time your sterilization with the food that you plan on canning to make sure that jars don't get to cool.

Never add hot food to a cool jar, because the glass jar will break. And viceversa don't add cold food to hot jars

Jar Packing

Since I mentioned in the above section about how to fill the jaw after you sterilize it, I thought it would be a great ideal and a help to you to go into detail about how to pack a jar when you get finish cleaning and sterilizing and your food once it is ready to be put inside the jar.

Raw packing

When raw packing a food item with boiling hot water, or if it is a fruit item you would want to cover it in a hot sugar syrup or juice. As I stated in the jar sterilizing reminder section you do not want to put cold food into a hot jar. Another step in raw packing is making sure that you leave enough head space between the food and the top of the can. This space will allow bubbling and prevents the overflow of the food items out of the can while you are doing the canning process. Most recipes calls for different measurements of headspace and is normally around 1/8 1/2 inch.

Hot Packing

To do hot packing you want to heat your food item in the boiling hot water before you put it into the jar, and a then you want put it in the sterilized jar. And you also want to make sure leave the appropriate headspace the recipe calls for.

Chapter 3: Fruit Butters

Pear Flavored Butter

Preparation Time: 15 Minutes | Cooking Time: 31 Minutes | Servings: 5

Ingredients:

- 4 Pounds of Pears, Medium in Size, Cored and Cut into Quarters
- 2 Cups of Sugar, White
- teaspoon of Orange Zest, Finely Grated
- 1/4 teaspoons of Nutmeg, Ground
- 1/4 Cup of Orange Juice, Fresh

Directions:

1. The first thing that you will want to do is place your pears into a large sized pot placed over medium heat. Add in water to cover your bears and cook until they are tender to the touch. This should take 30 minutes.
2. After this time remove your pears and press through a sieve, Hold onto your pulp.
3. Place your pear pulp into a large sized saucepan along with your sugar and stir thoroughly until your sugar fully dissolves.
4. Add in your remaining ingredients and cook this mixture over medium heat until it is thick in consistency. Cook for the next hour.
5. Pour your mixture into your canning jars and seal with your lids. Allow to cool completely.
6. Pour your mixture into your canning jars and seal with your lids.
7. Boil your jars in some boiling water for the next 10 minutes. Remove and allow to cool slightly before placing into your fridge. Use whenever you are ready.

Simple Cranberry Butter

Preparation Time: 5 Minutes | Cooking Time: 20 Minutes | Servings: 8

Ingredients:

- 2 Tablespoons of Cranberries, Dried
- 1/2 Cup of Water, Boiling
- 1/2 Cup of Butter, Soft to The Touch
- 3 Tablespoons of Sugar, Confectioner's Variety

Directions:

1. The first thing that you want to do is stir your boiling water and cranberries together in a large sized bowl. Allow to steep for the next 5 minutes.
2. After this time drain your cranberries and chop them finely.
3. Then use an electric mixer and beat your butter in a separate medium sized bowl until light and fluffy in texture.
4. Add in your sugar and cranberries and beat until thoroughly combined.
5. Pour your mixture into your canning jars and seal with your lids.
6. Boil your jars in some boiling water for the next 10 minutes. Remove and allow to cool slightly before placing into your fridge. Use whenever you are ready.

Classic Banana Jam

Preparation Time: 15 Minutes | Cooking Time: 15 Minutes | Servings: 15

Ingredients:

- 4 Cups of Bananas, Ripe
- 1/3 Cup of Lemon Juice, Fresh
- 2 Tablespoons of Brown Sugar, Light and Packed
- 1/4 teaspoons of Nutmeg, Ground

Directions:

1. Add all of your ingredients into a blender and blend on the highest setting until smooth in consistency.
2. Place into your canning jars and seal with your lids.
3. Boil your jars in some boiling water for the next 10 minutes. Remove and allow to cool slightly before placing into your fridge. Use whenever you are ready.

Acorn Squash Style Butter

Preparation Time: 5 Minutes | Cooking Time: 3 Hours | Servings: 8

Ingredients:

- 3 Acorn Squash, cut into Halves and Seeded
- teaspoon of Cinnamon, Ground
- 1 teaspoon of Nutmeg, Ground
- 1 teaspoon of Ginger, Ground
- 1/2 teaspoons of Cloves, Ground
- 1/4 Cups of Brown Sugar

- 1, 12 Ounce Can of Apple Juice, Concentrated, Frozen and Thawed

Directions:

1. The first thing that you want to do is preheat your oven to 400 degrees.
2. Next fill up 2 medium sized baking dishes with at least 1 inch of water. Then place your sliced acorn squash into your baking pan and place into your oven to bake until tender to the touch. This should take at least 1 hour. After this time remove and discard your water. Set aside to cool completely.
3. Scoop the flesh out from your squash and add into a blender. Blend on the highest setting until smooth in consistency.
4. Add in your next 4 ingredients and blend again to combine and until thick in consistency.
5. Spoon into a large sized saucepan. Add in your brown sugar and apple juice and continue to cook over medium heat for the next 40 to 45 minutes or until thick in consistency.
6. Remove from heat and allow to cool completely.
7. Pour your mixture into your canning jars and seal with your lids.
8. Boil your jars in some boiling water for the next 10 minutes. Remove and allow to cool slightly before placing into your fridge. Use whenever you are ready.

Healthy Chia Seed Jam

Preparation Time: 15 Minutes | Cooking Time: 35 Minutes | Servings: 15

Ingredients:

- 1/4 Cup of Chia Seeds
- 1/2 Cup of Water, Cold
- 2 Cups of Raspberries, Frozen
- 1/2 Cup of Blackberries, Frozen
- 1/2 Cup of Blueberries, Frozen
- 2 Strawberries, Frozen
- 1/3 Cup of Honey, Raw

Directions:

1. The first thing that you will want to do is soak your chia seeds in some water until it resembles a jelly like consistency. This should take about 5 minutes.
2. Then add in your berries and honey into a medium sized saucepan. Place over medium heat and cook until your berries are tender to the touch. This should take about 15 minutes.
3. After this time crush your berries thoroughly until smooth in consistency.
4. Next stir your chia seed mixture into your berry mixture until thoroughly combined.
5. Remove from heat and allow to cool completely.
6. Pour your mixture into your canning jars and seal with your lids.
7. Boil your jars in some boiling water for the next 10 minutes. Remove and allow to cool slightly before placing into your fridge. Use whenever you are ready.

Budget Friendly Berry Jam

Preparation Time: 5 Minutes | Cooking Time: 25 Minutes | Servings: 3

Ingredients:

- 4 Cups of Tomato Pulp, Green in Color
- 4 Cups of Sugar, White
- 2, 3 Ounce Packs of JellO, Your Favorite Kind

Directions:

1. First use a large sized saucepan placed over medium to high heat. Add in your tomato pulp and sugar and bring this mixture to a boil.
2. Once your mixture is boiling reduce the heat to low and cook for the next 20 minutes, making sure that you stir the mixture once in a while.
3. Remove your mixture from heat and add in your JellO, making sure to stir thoroughly to combine and until it completely dissolves. Allow your mixture to cool completely.
4. Pour your mixture into your canning jars and seal with your lids.
5. Boil your jars in some boiling water for the next 10 minutes. Remove and allow to cool slightly before placing into your fridge. Use whenever you are ready.

Pumpkin Butter

Preparation Time: 15 Minutes | Cooking Time: 30 minutes | Servings: 3

Ingredients:

- Pumpkin puree – 30 oz (canned or fresh)
- Granulated sugar – 1/2 cup
- Brown sugar – 1/2 cup
- 100% pure apple juice or apple cider – 1 cup
- Ground cinnamon – 2 tsp
- Ground ginger – 1 tsp
- Freshly grated whole nutmeg – 3/4tsp
- Ground cloves – 1/2 tsp
- Lemon juice – 2 tsp

Direction:

1. Combine all ingredients and cook on medium high for 2025 minutes until thick and spreadable.
2. Transfer to airtight container and refrigerate once cool.

Apple Banana Butter

Preparation Time: 5 Minutes | Cooking Time: 2 1/2 hours | Servings: 4

Ingredients:

- Apples – 2 lbs
- Bananas – 3
- Sugar – 3/4cup
- Water – 1 cup

Direction:

1. Combine all ingredients and cook for 2 hours.
2. Fill into jars.
3. Process in boilingwater canner for 7 minutes.

Apple Butter

Preparation Time: 15 Minutes | Cooking Time: 45 minutes | Servings: 4

Ingredients:

- Apples – 14
- Water – 2 cups

- Sugar – 3 cups
- Cinnamon – 3 tsp

Direction:

1. Core, peel and cut apples.
2. Combine apples with water and cook until soft. Puree.
3. Add sugar and cinnamon.
4. Boil over medium heat until it thickens.
5. Ladle into prepared jars and process in boilingwater canner for 10 minutes

Banana Butter

Preparation Time: 5 Minutes | Cooking Time: 30 Minutes | Servings: 4

Ingredients:

- Bananas – 5
- Chopped pineapple – 3 cups
- Desiccated coconut – 1/4 cup
- Sugar – 3 cups
- Lemon juice – 5 tsp
- Water – 1/4 cup

Direction:

1. Combine all ingredients in a pot and bring to a boil.
2. Cook until the mixture thickens.
3. Transfer into jars.
4. Process in boilingwater bath for 15 minutes.

Hot Pepper Mustard Butter

Preparation Time: 15 Minutes | Cooking Time: 1 hours | Servings: 9

Ingredients:

- 36 large hot peppers (or 50 small ones), washed and trimmed
- yellow bell pepper, seeded, chop in a few pieces
- 1 red onion, trimmed and quartered
- 1 quart of prepared yellow mustard
- 1 quart of cider vinegar
- 6 cups of sugar
- 1 1/4 cup of flour
- 1 1/2 cups of water
- 1 teaspoon of salt

Directions

1.   Place hot peppers, bell pepper and onion in the food processor and pulse until finely minced.

2.   Mix all of the ingredients together in a large saucepan. Bring to a boil while stirring continuously. Reduce heat to low and let simmer for 15 minutes, stirring a few times.

3.   Put into hot sterilized jars, put the lids on, and let them sit in a water bath for about 10 minutes.

4.   Let cool completely before storing.

Chapter 4: Pickles

Watermelon Style Pickles

Preparation Time: 15 Minutes | Cooking Time: 21 Hours and 15 Minutes | Servings: 7

Ingredients:

- Cup of Salt, Canning Variety
- 1 Gallon of Water, Cold
- 16 Cups of Watermelon Rind, Cut into Cubes
- 1 Gallon of Water, Cold
- Sticks of Cinnamon
- 1 teaspoon of Allspice, Whole
- 1 teaspoon of Cloves, Whole
- Cups of Vinegar, White
- Cups of Sugar, White
- 12 Cherries, Maraschino Variety and Cut into Halves
- 6, 1 Pint Canning Jars, With Lids and Rings

Directions:

1. Put into hot sterilized jars, put the lids on, and let them sit in a water bath for about 10 minutes.
2. Let cool completely before storing.
3. The first thing that you will want to do is stir your salt into your gallon of water in a large sized container until it is completely dissolved. Add in your watermelon rind then cover with

some plastic wrap and allow to sit for the next 12 hours. After this time drain and rinse completely.
4. Next place your remaining gallon of water and watermelon rind into a large sized stock pot. Set over medium heat and bring to a boil. Once boiling reduce the heat to low and continue to simmer for the next 45 minutes to an hour or until your rind is tender to the touch.
5. Add in your next 3 ingredients into a spice bag and submerge into your pot.
6. Add in your remaining ingredients and stir to combine. Reduce the heat to low and allow to simmer for the next 5 to 10 minutes.
7. After this time remove your spice bag and remove your mixture from heat. Allow to cool completely.
8. Pour your mixture into your canning jars and seal with your lids.
9. Boil your jars in some boiling water for the next 10 minutes. Remove and allow to cool slightly before placing into your fridge. Use whenever you are ready.

Garlic Flavored Pickles

Preparation Time: 5 Minutes | Cooking Time: 8 Hours and 5 Minutes | Servings: 7

Ingredients:

- 16 Ounce Jar of Pickles, Dill Variety
- 2 Cups of Sugar, White
- tablespoon of Hot Sauce, Your Favorite Kind
- 6 Cloves of Garlic, Peeled and Minced
- 1/4 teaspoons of Red Pepper Flakes, Crushed

Directions::

1. Place your canned dill pickles and the liquid into a large sized bowl.
2. Add in your remaining ingredients and stir thoroughly to combine.
3. Pour your mixture into your pickle jar and seal with your lid.
4. Boil your jars in some boiling water for the next 10 minutes. Remove and allow to cool slightly before placing into your fridge. Use whenever you are ready.

Quick Pickles

Preparation Time: 15 Minutes | Cooking Time: 5 hours (including wait time) | Servings: 8

Ingredients:

- Cucumbers – 6 lbs
- Onions – 3 lbs
- Pickling salt – 1/2 cup
- Vinegar – 4 cups
- Sugar – 4 1/2 cups
- Mustard seeds – 2 tbsp
- Celery seeds – 1 1/2 tbsp.
- Ground turmeric – 1 tbsp

Direction:

1. Wash and chop cucumbers and onions.
2. Combine cucumbers and onions in a bowl with salt.
3. Cover with ice and refrigerate for 5 hours, adding more ice when necessary.
4. Drain the water out.
5. Combine remaining ingredients in a pot and boil for 10 minutes.
6. Add cucumbers and onions and boil for 3 more minutes.
7. Fill hot jars with the concoction and seal tight.
8. Let it sit undisturbed for 45 weeks

Garlic Dill Pickles

Preparation Time: 5 Minutes | Cooking Time: 30 Minutes | Servings: 4

Ingredients:

- Cucumbers – 10
- Vinegar – 2 cups
- Water – 2 cups
- Salt – 2 tbsp
- Dill seeds – 2 tbsp
- Garlic – 6 cloves
- Peppercorns – 2 tsp

Direction:

1. Chop the cucumbers.
2. Combine vinegar, water and salt and boil.
3. Separate the garlic, dill seeds and peppercorns equally between the jars.
4. Pack the cucumbers tightly into the jars.
5. Pour the hot liquid into the jars.
6. Process in boilingwater bath for 10 minutes.

Jalapeno Rings

Preparation Time: 15 Minutes | Cooking Time: 20 Minutes | Servings: 6

Ingredients:

- Jalapeno peppers – 10
- Water – 3/4cup

- Vinegar – 3/4cup
- Granulated sugar – 3 tbsp
- Salt – 1 tbsp
- Oregano – 1 tsp

Direction:

1. Combine all ingredients except peppers and bring to a rolling boil.
2. Pack jalapeno peppers into jars.
3. Pour hot vinegar mixture onto peppers.

Pickled Beets

Preparation Time: 15 Minutes | Cooking Time: 2 hours | Servings: 5

Ingredients:

- Beets – 6
- Sugar – 2 cups
- Vinegar – 1 1/2 cups
- Water – 2 1/2 cups
- Salt – 1 tbsp
- Cloves – 1/4 cup

Direction:

1. Cover chopped beets in water and cook for 30 minutes, until soft.
2. Combine sugar, water, cloves, and vinegar and boil for 10 minutes.
3. Fill the beets into jars and pour boiling water on top.
4. Process in boilingwater canner for 10 minutes.

Bread and Butter Pickles

Preparation Time: 5 Minutes | Cooking Time: 20 minutes | Servings: 3

Ingredients:

- 15 cups of sliced pickling cucumbers, about 5 pounds; three cups for every pound
- 3 onions sliced thinly
- 1/4 cup of salt
- 2 1/2 cups of cider vinegar
- 2 1/2 cups of sugar
- 3/4teaspoon of turmeric
- 1/2 teaspoon of celery seed
- tablespoon of mustard seeds
- 6 cups of water

Directions

1. Mix the onions, ice, salt, and cucumbers together in a bowl.
2. Place a plate on top of the bowl with a gallon of water or something heavy on the plate. This serves as a weight. Let it stand for about three hours.
3. After three hours, rinse, and then drain.
4. Mix the sugar, vinegar, celery seed, mustard seed, and turmeric together in a large pot.
5. Add the drained cucumbers.
6. Bring the 6 cups of water almost to a boil in a pot on medium heat.
7. Right at boiling, remove from heat, and seal in the sterilized jars,
8. Place in a hot water bath for 10 minutes.
9. Dry them off, and place on a cookie sheet right side up for around 15 minutes in the oven at 225°F. This is done in order to ensure that there are no air pockets, that everything has been cooked right, and that it is sterilized and sealed properly before being stored. Let cool completely before storing.

Pickled Green Beans

Preparation Time: 15 Minutes | Cooking Time: 2 hours | Servings: 6

Ingredients:

- 4 pounds of green beans
- 5 teaspoons of crushed red pepper flakes

- 5 teaspoons of mustard seeds
- 5 teaspoons of dill seeds
- 10 cloves of garlic, one per jar
- 5 cups of water
- 5 cups of vinegar
- 1/3 cup of salt

Directions

1. Wash green beans, and cut them to fit into the jars you have.
2. Mix the red pepper flakes, mustard seeds, dill seeds, and cloves of garlic and put an equal amount into each jar while you bring the water, vinegar, and salt to a boil.
3. Pour the boiling liquids over the beans, tighten the lids, and let the jars sit in a water bath 5 minutes.
4. Let cool completely before storing.

Pickled Peppers

Preparation Time: 5 Minutes | Cooking Time: 10 Minutes | Servings: 4

Ingredients:

- 4 cups white vinegar
- 2 water cups
- 2 tablespoons sugar
- Olive oil

- onion, medium diced
- mediumsized carrots, medium diced
- Peppers
- Dried oregano
- Bay leaves

Directions:

1. Mix together the vinegar, water, and sugar in a medium saucepan and heat until the mixture reaches a simmer.
2. Meanwhile, sauté the onions and carrots in olive oil until tender.
3. Using pintsized canning jars, place approximately 1 tablespoon of the mixture in the bottom of a jar, then add the peppers (if you make 3 small incisions on each pepper, the flavors of the brine will infuse more quickly).
4. Add one bay leaf and 1/2 teaspoon of oregano to each jar. Seal the jars, and process in a hot water bath for 10 minutes.
5. The flavor for these peppers will be best after at least two weeks.

Chunky Zucchini Pickles

Preparation Time: 15 Minutes | Cooking Time: 35 Minutes | Servings: 4

Ingredients:

- 14 cups seeded, unpeeled zucchini (I peeled half of them because this zucchini was huge and the skin was tougher than smaller zucchini)
- 6 cups finely chopped onions
- 1/4 cup pickling or canning salt
- 3 cups granulated sugar
- 4 tbsp. Clearjel (I have never seen this in stores but you can purchase it online ~ I used 2 tbsp. of corn starch)
- 1/4 cup dry mustard
- tbsp. ground ginger
- 1 tsp. ground turmeric
- 1/2 cup water
- cups white vinegar
- 1 red bell pepper, seeded and finely chopped

Directions:

1. In a large glass or stainless steel bowl, combine zucchini and onions. Sprinkle with pickling

salt, cover, and let stand at room temperature for 1 hour. Transfer to a colander placed over a sink and drain thoroughly. Note: I also rinsed half the mixture because that is what I've done in the past with pickles…but it says DRAIN not rinse. They still seemed salty.

2. Prepare for waterbath canning. Sterilize jars in the oven on 250F for 30 minutes.

3. In a large stainless steel saucepan, combine sugar, Clearjel or corn starch, mustard, ginger, and turmeric. Stir dry ingredients well. Gradually blend in water. Add vinegar and red pepper.

4. Bring to a boil over mediumhigh heat, stirring frequently to dissolve sugar and prevent lumps from forming. Reduce heat and boil gently, stirring frequently, until mixture thickens about 5 minutes. Add drained zucchini mixture and return to a boil.

5. Ladle hot zucchini mixture into hot sterilized jars, leaving 1/2 headspace. Remove air bubbles and adjust headspace, if necessary, by adding more hot zucchini mixture. Wipe rim with a damp paper towel. Place snaps and rings on each jar, screwing bands down until they are fingertiptight.

6. Place jars in canner, ensuring they are completely covered with water. Bring to a full rolling boil and process for 10 minutes. When time is up, turn off the heat, remove canner lid and wait 5 minutes before removing jars to a folded towel on the counter.

7. Check seals, label, and store. Refrigerate any unsealed jars.

Pickled Brussels Sprouts

Preparation Time: 5 Minutes | Cooking Time: 10 Minutes | Servings: 4

Ingredients:

- 3 lbs. fresh Brussels sprouts halved
- medium sweet red pepper, finely chopped
- 6 garlic cloves, halved
- 1 medium onion, thinly sliced
- tsp. crushed red pepper flakes
- 1 tbsp. celery seed
- 1 tbsp. whole peppercorns
- tbsp. canning salt
- 1/2 sugar cup

- 21/2 white vinegar cups
- 21/2 water cups

Directions:

1. Fill a Dutch oven threefourths full with water; bring to a boil.
2. Add Brussels sprouts in batches, cooking, uncovered, 4 minutes until tendercrisp.
3. With a slotted spoon remove and drop into ice water. Drain and pat dry.
4. Pack Brussels sprouts into six hot 1pint jars.
5. Divide garlic and pepper flakes among jars.
6. In a large saucepan, bring remaining ingredients to a boil.
7. Carefully scoop the hot liquid over Brussels sprouts, leaving 1/4inch space of the top. Remove air bubbles and if necessary, adjust headspace by adding hot mixture. Wipe the rims carefully. Place tops on jars and screw on bands until fingertip tight.
8. Place jars into canner with simmering water, ensuring that they are completely covered with water. Let boil for 10 minutes. Remove jars and cool.

Pickled Peaches

Preparation Time: 5 Minutes | Cooking Time: 30 Minutes | Servings: 4

Ingredients:

- 3 pounds of peaches that have been peeled, pitted and cut in halves
- Three cups of sugar
- One and threequarter cups of white vinegar

- A cinnamon stick (2 inches)
- One teaspoon of whole cloves
- One teaspoon of juniper berries

Directions

1. Combine the sugar and the vinegar in a large stainless steel pot. Bring the mixture to a boil; stir the sugar in until it dissolves completely.
2. Combine the cinnamon, clove and juniper berries in a spice bag or a spice ball. Add the spice ball and peaches to the mixture in the stainless steel pot.
3. Allow the mixture to simmer for ten minutes – or until the peaches are cooked. Make sure that the peaches aren't too soft. Stir the peaches tenderly to ensure that they cook on all sides.
4. Cover the pot and let it stand in a cool area – not the fridge – for three hours. Stir the peaches a couple of times during this period.
5. Return the pot to the stove and heat the peaches, bringing them to a boil, for two minutes.
6. Remove the pot from the heat and remove the spice ball form the pot.
7. Remove the jars from the simmering pot and place them on a towel. Use a canning funnel to pour the peaches into your jars. Leave one and a half inches of headspace.
8. Use a damp cloth to clean the rims of the jars. Seal the lids and apply the bands, adjusting them until they are as tight as possible.
9. Place your jars in the canning rack and make sure the jars are covered by one to two inches. Cover the canner with its lid.
10. Processing time for this recipe is twenty minutes.
11. Remove the jars from the pot and place them on a towel. Allow the jars to cool overnight.
12. Test the lids for sealing and store the sealed jars in a cool, dry storage space.

Salt Pickles

Preparation Time: 15 Minutes | Cooking Time: 2 hours | Servings: 6

Ingredients:

- Plain water – Half a gallon

- Grain vinegar – One cup
- Canning salt – Half a cup
- Sugar – quarter cup

Directions

1. You need to mix the sugar and the salt and then dissolve them in your water
2. Next add your vinegar
3. Now let your solution cool down
4. Now take your cucumbers, your dill as well as your herbs of hot pepper, grape leaves as well as garlic, and put them all in one jar.
5. Next pour your vinegar mixture when it has cooled down in the jar with cucumbers and put on the lid. From this point, you need to wait for around 5 or 6 days and your salt pickles will be done.

Peanut Pickles

Preparation Time: 5 Minutes | Cooking Time: 10 Minutes | Servings: 4

Ingredients:

- Sugar – 2 cups
- Corn syrup that is light – 1 cup
- Plain water – 1/4 cup
- Salted peanuts – 11/2 cups
- Butter – 3 tablespoon
- Vanilla – 1 teaspoon
- Baking soda – 2 teaspoon

Directions

1. Mix the sugar and corn syrup first in a saucepan
2. Add your water to that mixture

3. After you have mixed your contents well, heat it and ensure to use medium heat as you stir the contents
4. Continue with the process till the heat in your mixture is 285° Fahrenheit.
5. Now add in the peanuts plus the butter and begin to stir the contents. When the contents have reached 295° Fahrenheit, get the saucepan off the fire.
6. It is at this point that you add your vanilla plus the baking soda and then proceed to stir your contents. You need to mix till you can see foam.
7. Take a buttered pan and pour in the mixture, and let it sit for between 8 and 10 minutes
8. Pick a knife and mark squares in your content
9. When the brittle looks like it is cool, invert your pan and tap it off the pan
10. You can even proceed to cut your brittle into pieces according to your guiding squares.

Mustard Pickled Vegetables

Preparation Time: 15 Minutes | Cooking Time: 15 minutes | Servings: 4

Ingredients:

- head cauliflower
- 20 small green tomatoes
- green bell peppers
- cups pickling onions
- 2 pickling cucumbers
- 1 cup sugar
- 3/4cup flour
- 1/2 cup dry mustard 1 tbsp. turmeric
- 7 cups apple cider vinegar
- 7 cups water
- 1 cup pickling salt

Directions:

1. Wash all the veggies and chop.
2. Toss the vegetables in a large nonreactive bowl or pot with salt.
3. Pour a quart of water over all of them and let this stand overnight.
4. Drain, cover with boiling water, and let it stand for ten minutes. Drain.
5. Combine sugar, flour, spices, vinegar, and 3 cups of water, then cook until thick.
6. Mix in the veggies and cook until tendercrisp.
7. Pack into pint jars, dividing liquid evenly and leaving 1/2inch of headspace.
8. Wipe rims; screw on lids and rings.
9. Finish the canning process in a boiling water bath for 15 minutes.

Dill Pickles

Preparation Time: 5 Minutes | Cooking Time: 60 Minutes | Servings: 4

Ingredients:

- 4 cups of water
- 3 cups of vinegar
- 12 head fresh dill and leaves
- 4 lbs of pickling cucumbers
- 8 cloves of garlic, peeled (Optional)
- 8 small hot chili peppers (also optional)
- 1/4 cup of pickling salt
- 4 tsp of mixed pickling spice

Directions:

1. First, start by scrubbing the cucumbers thoroughly and cut about 1/4 inch slice off the blossom end.
2. Then, prepare the preserving jars.

3. Add water and vinegar into the sauce pan and bring to a boil
4. Reduce heat but keep it at a simmer
5. Work on one jar at a time, add 3 dill heads and some leaves, 2 garlic cloves, 2 hot peppers, 1tbsp salt, and 1tsp pickling spice in the jar.
6. Pack the cucumbers in the jar, wedge them in so none of them floats to the top, give it one inch of head space. Then, pour in the hot vinegar solution, giving it about 1/4 inch headspace.

Tarragon Pickled Green Beans

Preparation Time: 15 Minutes | Cooking Time: 2 hours | Servings: 5

Ingredients:

- 6 cloves of garlic, thinly sliced
- 36 whole peppercorns, crushed
- 3 lbs of green beans, washed and trimmed to 4 inches
- 6 sprigs of fresh tarragon, can be substituted with 12 basil sprigs
- 3 1/2 cups of white wine vinegar, or just white vinegar
- 3 1/2 cups of water
- 2 tbsp of pickling salt or kosher salt

Directions:

1. Process the lids
2. Then, divide the garlic and pepper corns into 6 pint jars
3. Pack the green beans into the jars tightly and add sprigs of tarragon/basil

4. Heat the water, vinegar, and salt to boil at medium heat. Pour over the green beans in the jars, give it 1/2 inch headspace.
5. Process for 5 minutes in boiling water. Remove and let cool. You should hear the ping as it cools.

Pickled Curry Cauliflower

Preparation Time: 5 Minutes | Cooking Time: 45 Minutes | Servings: 4

Ingredients:

- 1/2 tbsp canning salt
- 4 cups vinegar
- cups water
- tsp cumin seeds
- tsp turmeric
- 3 tsp curry powder
- lbs cauliflower
- Serrano peppers

Directions:

6. With a 4quart kettle, combine the water, salt, and vinegar. Bring to a simmer over mediumlow heat and whisk to help dissolve the salt. Keep hot until ready to use.
7. Pack jars with cauliflower. Add 1/2 tsp of cumin seeds, turmeric, and curry flower, and 1 Serrano pepper into each jar.
8. Pour hot brine into the jars, leaving 1/2 inch headspace.
9. Process for 12 minutes.
10. Remove from water, let cool for 12 hours.

Spicy Dill Pickles

Preparation Time: 15 Minutes | Cooking Time: 1 hours | Servings: 5

Ingredients:

- 1/2 tsp red pepper flakes
- 10 cloves garlic, peeled and smashed
- 5 tsp dill seed, separated
- 2 tbsp canning salt
- 3 tbsp honey
- 4 cups water
- cup white vinegar

- cups apple cider vinegar
- 11 lbs cucumber

Directions:

1. Combine both kinds of vinegar, honey, salt, and water. Bring to a boil, then reduce to a simmer.
2. Cut 1/2 inch off each end of the cucumbers and discard. Slice 1/4inch slices and set aside. If you are not using fresh cucumber, soak in ice water for 2 hours first.
3. Add one smashed garlic clove, and one hot pepper or 1/2 red pepper flakes in each jar. Pack cucumbers in, give it 1/2 inch headspace. Add 1/2 tsp dill seed on top.
4. Pour brine over, giving the same headspace.
5. Process your jars in boiling water for 10 minutes.
6. Remove and let cool naturally for 12 hours. Then, store in a dark and dry place for two weeks before consumption or storage.

Spiced Beets

Preparation Time: 5 Minutes | Cooking Time: 60 Minutes | Servings: 4

Ingredients:

- 1/4 tsp. salt
- 3/4 tsp. allspice
- 3/4 tsp. cloves
- 1/4 stick cinnamon
- 1/4 piece mace
- 1-1/2 tsps. celery seed
- 2 cups cider vinegar, 5% acidity
- cup sugar
- pints beets

Directions

1. Tie the salt and the spices in a thin cloth bag. Boil the vinegar, sugar, and spices for 15 minutes. Sterilize a quart jar for 15 minutes. Remove the jar from the water and pour in the vinegar mix. Fix the lid and set aside for 2 weeks.
2. Remove the spice bag. Cook fresh beets until tender but firm, and let cool. Peel the beets. Heat the vinegar and add 1/2 cup of the beet

liquid. Add the beets and simmer for 15 minutes.
3. Pack into sterile jars, being sure the vinegar covers the beets. Remove air bubbles and adjust the lids. Process for 10 minutes in a boiling water bath.

Spicy Carrots

Preparation Time: 5 Minutes | Cooking Time: 60 Minutes | Servings: 4

Ingredients:

- 1/4 tsp. salt
- 3/4 tsp. allspice
- 3/4 tsp. cloves
- 1/4 stick cinnamon
- 1/4 piece mace
- 1-1/2 tsps. celery seed
- 2 cups cider vinegar, 5% acidity
- cup sugar
- pints carrots

Directions

1. Tie the salt and the spices in thin cloth bag. Boil the vinegar, sugar, and spices for 15 minutes. Sterilize a quart jar for about 15 minutes in boiling water. Remove the jar from the water and pour in the vinegar mix. Fix the lid and set aside for 2 weeks.
2. Remove the spice bag. Cook fresh carrots until tender but firm, and let cool. Heat the vinegar and add 1/2 cup of the carrot liquid. Add the carrots and simmer for 15 minutes.
3. Pack into sterile jars, being sure the vinegar covers the carrots. Remove air bubbles and

adjust the lids. Process 10 minutes in a boiling water bath.

Canned Green Beans

Preparation Time: 5 Minutes | Cooking Time: 20 Minutes | Servings: 4

Ingredients:

- 10 lbs string beans
- Canning salt, optional

Directions:

1. Rinse the beans, remove string, trim ends, and cut into 1-inch pieces
2. Put the beans into jars, leaving 1 inch headspace. If using canning salt, add 1/2 tsp per pint jar.
3. Put in boiling water, maintaining headspace.
4. Process jars under 10 pounds pressure for 20 minutes, adjust for altitude if needed.
5. Let cool for 12 hours and remove.

Sweet Carrots

Preparation Time: 5 Minutes | Cooking Time: 28 Minutes | Servings: 4

Ingredients:

- 3 tbsp pickling spice
- 2 tsp canning salt
- 2 cups sugar
- cup water
- 5 1/2 cups white distilled vinegar 5%
- 8 1/2 cups small carrots, peeled

Directions:

1. Wash small carrots and peel if desired, and set aside.
2. Combine everything else in a large stockpot and bring to a boil. Boil for 3 minutes.
3. Add carrots and bring to a boil. Then, reduce to a simmer and heat for 10 minutes, or until half-cooked. Then remove.
4. Ladle carrots into jars, leaving 1 inch headspace. Pour pickling spice in, leaving 1/2 inch headspace.
5. Process for 15 minutes, adjust for altitude.
6. Let cool for 12 hours and remove.

Blue Ribbon Green Beans

Preparation Time: 15 Minutes | Cooking Time: 40 Minutes | Servings: 1

Ingredients:

- 1/2 to 3/4 lbs green bush beans per pint
- 1/2 tsp salt per pint, optional

Directions:

1. Wash and snap the beans to fit jars
2. Raw pack beans into jars
3. In a pan, bring water to a boil, and add salt if desired. Stir to dissolve.
4. Pour boiling into jars over the beans, leaving 1 inch headspace.
5. Process jars for 20 minutes at 10 pounds of pressure for 20 minutes.
6. Let cool for 12 hours and remove.

Dried Beans

Preparation Time: 10 Minutes | Cooking Time: 12 hours and 30 Minutes | Servings: 2

Ingredients:

- 3 1/4 lbs dried beans
- Canning salt, optional
- cup Water

Directions:

1. Rinse the beans well, add to a large pot and add water until submerged under at least 2 inches of water. Cover and soak for 12 hours overnight.
2. Drain the beans and rinse well, add to a clean pot with the same amount of freshwater. Bring to boil, then reduce to a simmer for 30 minutes. Stir occasionally.
3. Fill jars with beans, leaving 1 inch headspace. Process at 10 pounds pressure for 75 minutes. Let cool for 12-24 hours before removal and storage.

Green Tomatoes

Preparation Time: 25 Minutes | Cooking Time: 30 Minutes | Servings: 4

Ingredients:

- 6 Fresno chile peppers, divided the long way
- 4 narrows clears out
- 1/4 cup coriander seeds
- 1/4 cup cumin seeds
- 2 cinnamon sticks
- 2 teaspoons entire cloves
- 2 teaspoons ground mace
- 4 tablespoons dark peppercorns
- 10 cloves garlic
- 8 cups juice vinegar
- 1/2 cup nectar
- 4 tablespoons genuine salt
- 4 pounds green tomatoes

Direction:

1. Clean the jugs. Wash the jugs and covers in hot lathery water; flush well. Place a wire rack or discharge fish jars in the pot to keep the cups from touching the base. Fill the pot most of the way with water and convey to a stew (don't boil). Submerge the cups in the water and let stew until you're prepared to fill. Sanitize the tops in a different little pot of stewing water.
2. Make the salt water. Join the chilies, narrows leaves, coriander and cumin seeds, cinnamon sticks, cloves, mace, peppercorns, garlic, vinegar, nectar, salt and 1 cup water in a vast pan. Heat to the point of boiling; cook for 3 minutes. Cool somewhat. Expel the chilies and straight leaves with an opened spoon
3. Pack the tomatoes. Cut the tomatoes into wedges utilizing a cleaned blade and cutting board. Expel the jugs and tops from the stewing water with a jug lifter or tongs; load with the tomatoes and a few chilies and straight takes off
4. Fill and close. Pour the warm pickling fluid over the tomatoes in every jug, ceasing 1/2 inch from the top. Slide a spotless elastic spatula around within every cup to expel air boils. Wipe the edges with a perfect towel, then position the cleaned covers on top. Screw the tops close, being mindful so as not to overtighten.
5. Heat up the jugs. Return the pot of water to a stew; include the cups, ensuring water covers them by a couple inches. Cover and boil for 15 to 20 minutes. Turn off the warmth, reveal and abandon them in the water for 10 minutes
6. Evacuate and let cool. Exchange the cups to a kitchen towel. Let sit, undisturbed, for no less than 12 hours. A vacuum seal will frame as the jugs cool

Tasty Bread with Butter Pickles

Preparation Time: 25 Minutes | Cooking Time: 30 Minutes | Servings: 3

Ingredients:

For each 2 quarts of pickles:

- 3 1/2 lbs pickling cucumbers (around 14 little to medium)
- 2 1/2 cups vinegar (5% acridity)
- 2 1/2 cups sugar
- 1/4 cup Ball Bread and Butter Pickle Mix
- 2 Ball Quart (32 oz) Fresh Preserving cups with covers and bands
- Optional: Ball freshTECH Electric Water Bath Canner + Multicooker

Directions:

1. Cut finishes off cucumbers. Cut into 1/2 inch cuts.
2. Mix vinegar, sugar, and ball® bread and butter pickle mix in a medium pan. Warmth to a boil.
3. Pack in view of enjoy now or fresh preserve ventures beneath.
4. Enjoy baking powder now (refrigerate up to 3 months):
5. Pour hot pickling fluid over cucumber cuts in a heavydish. Cool to room temperature, around 30 minutes.
6. Pack cucumber cuts into cups. Spoon pickling fluid over cucumbers. Place tops and bands on cups.
7. Refrigerate pickles. For best flavor, permit pickles to remain in icebox for 3 weeks.

Watermelon Rind Pickles

Preparation Time: 5 Minutes | Cooking Time: 15 Minutes | Servings: 5

Ingredients:

- 8 cups of sliced peeled watermelon rind (2x1-in. pieces)
- 6 cups of water
- cup of canning salt
- 4 cups of sugar
- cups of white vinegar
- 6 cinnamon sticks (3 inches), divided
- 1 tsp whole cloves
- 1 tsp whole peppercorns

Directions:

1. In a large nonreactive dish, mix the rind, water, and salt. Refrigerate for several hours or overnight in the refrigerator. Rinse and drain well. 2 cinnamon sticks, cloves, and peppercorns in a Dutch oven. Bring the water to a boil. Return to a boil with the rinds. Decrease heat to low and cook 10 minutes, uncovered or until vegetables are soft.
2. Remove the cinnamon sticks and throw them away. Fill 4 heated 1-pint jars halfway with hot mixture, leaving 1/2-inch headspace. Fill every jar with the remaining cinnamon stick. Remove air bubbles and, if necessary, correct headspace by adding heated mixture. Clean the rims.
3. Screw on bands until fingertip tight; center lids on jars. Place the jars in a canner filled with simmering water, making sure they are completely covered. Take a boil and reduce to a frying glass minutes. Set the jars aside to cool.

Pickled Peveryes

Preparation Time: 15 Minutes | Cooking Time: 25 Minutes | Servings: 7

Ingredients:

- 6 cinnamon sticks (3 inches)
- 24 whole peppercorns
- 18 whole cloves
- 2 tsp thinly sliced fresh ginger root
- 12 medium peveryes, peeled, pitted and quartered
- 3 cups of sugar

- cup of white vinegar
- 1 cup of water

Directions:

1. Add peveryes to 6 heated pint jars with cinnamon sticks, peppercorns, cloves, and ginger pieces. Bring to a boil sugar, vinegar and water in a big pot. Ladle boiling liquid over peveryes with care, leaving 1/2-inch headspace.
2. Remove air bubbles and, if necessary, correct headspace by adding heated mixture. Clean the rims. Screw on bands until fingertip tight; center lids on jars. Place the jars in a canner filled with simmering water, making sure they are completely covered.
3. Take a boil and reduce to a frying glass for 15 Ten minutes. Ten minutes. Remove and chill the jars. Remove them.

Sweet & Spicy Pickled Red Seedless Grapes

Preparation Time: 5 Minutes | Cooking Time: 28 Minutes | Servings: 8

Ingredients:

- 5 cups of seedless red grapes
- 4 jalapeno peppers, seeded and sliced
- 2 tbsp minced fresh gingerroot
- 2 cinnamon sticks (3 inches), halved
- 4 whole star anise
- 2 tsp coriander seeds
- 2 tsp mustard seed
- 2 cups of packed brown sugar
- 2 cups of white wine vinegar
- cup of water
- 1 cup of dry red wine
- 1-1/2 tsp canning salt

Directions:

1. Fill four heated 1-pint jars with grapes to within 1-1/2 inch of the top. Fill jars halfway with jalapenos, ginger, cinnamon, star anise, coriander seeds, and mustard seeds. Mix brown sugar, vinegar, water, wine, and canning salt in a big pot. Bring to a boil, simmer for around 15-18 minutes, or until liquid is reduced to 3 cups of.

2. Ladle boiling liquid over grape mixture with care, leaving 1/2-inch headspace. Remove air bubbles and, if necessary, correct headspace by adding hot liquid. Clean the rims. Screw on bands until fingertip tight; center lids on jars. Place the jars in the canner, making sure they are thoroughly submerged. Take a boil and reduce to a frying glass for 10 minutes. Remove the jars and set them aside to cool.

Sweet and Sour Zucchini Pickles

Preparation Time: 5 Minutes | Cooking Time: 15 Minutes | Servings: 7

Ingredien

- 11 cups of thinly sliced zucchini (about 3 pounds)
- large onion, halved and thinly sliced
- 1/3 cup of canning salt
- 4-1/2 cups of white vinegar
- cups of sugar
- 1 tbsp mustard seed
- 1-1/2 tsp ground turmeric

Directions:

1. In a large nonreactive bowl, mix the zucchini and onion. Toss in a pinch of salt and toss to coat. Cover with water and set aside for 2 hours at room temperature. Drain, rinse, and drain completely.
2. Mix the remaining ingredients in a 6-quart stockpot. Bring to a hot boil and stir constantly to dissolve the sugar. Slow to low heat and cook for 5 minutes. to enable flavors to meld.
3. Return to a boil, stirring periodically, with the zucchini mixture. Reduce cook and heat to low, uncovered, 4-5 minutes, or until well heated. Fill six hot 1-pint jars halfway with the heated Mix, leaving a headspace of 1/2-inch. Remove bubbles from the air and correct head space needed by adding hot pickling liquid. Clean the rims.
4. Screw on bands until fingertip tight; center lids on jars. Place the jars in a canner filled with simmering water, making sure they are completely covered. Take a boil and reduce to a frying glass for 10 minutes. Remove the jars and set them aside to cool.

Chapter 5: Marmalades & Preserves

Ginger Flavored Marmalade

Preparation Time: 15 Minutes | Cooking Time: 8 Hours and 35 MinutesServings: 32

Ingredients:

- 3 1/2 Cups of Ginger, Fresh and Peeled
- 4 Cups of Water, Cold
- 5 Cups of Sugar, White
- 1, 3 Ounce Package of Pectin, Liquid Variety
- 5, 1/2 Pint Canning Jars, With Lids and Jars

Directions::

1. First place your ginger and water into a large sized saucepan. Set over medium heat and bring this mixture to a boil.
2. Once your mixture is boiling reduce the heat to low. Cover and allow to simmer for the next hour and 15 minutes or until your ginger is tender to the touch.
3. Once tender strain your ginger through a fine mesh strainer and drain.
4. Place your ginger into a large sized bowl with your ginger liquid and allow to cool.
5. Place back into your large sized saucepan and add in your sugar. Boil for the next minute, making sure you stir constantly.
6. Add in your liquid pectin and reduce the heat to low. Continue to cook for the next 7 minutes and skim off any excess foam that may form on the top. Remove from heat and allow to cool completely.
7. Pour your mixture into your canning jars and seal with your lids.

8. Boil your jars in some boiling water for the next 10 minutes. Remove and allow to cool slightly before placing into your fridge. Use whenever you are ready.

Canned Asparagu

Preparation Time: 5 Minutes | Cooking Time: 30 minutes | Servings: 3

Ingredients:

- Asparagus – 20
- Salt – 2 tbsp
- Water – 5 cups
- Chili flakes – 1 tbsp
- Sugar – 1/4 cup

Direction:

1. Chop asparagus finely and boil for 5 minutes.
2. Combine sugar, vinegar, salt, and water.
3. Boil until sugar dissolves.
4. Pack tightly into jars.
5. Pour sugar mixture into jars.
6. Process in boilingwater canner for 10 minutes.

Rhubarb

Preparation Time: 15 Minutes | Cooking Time: 30 Minutes | Servings: 75

Ingredients:

- Sliced rhubarb – 1 1/2 cups
- Sugar – 1 1/2 cups

Direction:

1. Combine rhubarb and sugar until the juices start flowing.
2. Bring to a gentle boil and stir constantly.
3. Ladle into prepared jars and process in boiling water canner for 15 minutes

Peach Preserve

Preparation Time: 5 Minutes | Cooking Time: 45 minutes | Servings: 4

Ingredients:

- Peaches – 15
- Sugar – 4 cups
- Pectin – 2 oz

Direction:

1. Add chopped peaches and bring to a boil over mediumlow heat for 15 minutes until peaches soften.
2. Add sugar and boil once again until the mixture thickens.
3. Transfer into prepared jars and process in boilingwater canner for 10 minutes.

Pink Grapefruit Marmalade

Preparation Time: 5 Minutes | Cooking Time: 120 minutes | Servings: 4

Ingredients:

- 2 grapefruits
- 2 1/2 cups of sugar
- 2 1/2 cups of brown sugar

- 2 lemons, for the juice

Directions

1. Place the grapefruit in a pot with enough water so they can float freely.
2. Let them boil for about two hours, then let them cool.
3. Slice the grapefruit and mix with the sugars and lemon juice.
4. Place back into pot and bring to a boil and let sit for about 15 minutes.
5. Put into jars and let the jars sit for about 10 minutes.
6. Let cool completely before storing.

Peaches and Vanilla Syrup

Preparation Time: 15 Minutes | Cooking Time: 2 hours | Servings: 4

Ingredients:

- 5 cups of peaches, pureed
- 2 cups of sugar
- 2 tablespoons of lemon juice
- 2 teaspoons of vanilla

Directions

1. Mix peach puree with sugar and lemon juice in a mediumsized sauce pot, and bring to a boil.
2. Let it simmer for about five minutes, and then add the vanilla.
3. Pour the mixture into jars, and seal them.
4. Let the jars sit in a water bath for about 20 minutes before storing.
5. Let cool completely before storing.

Spicy Roasted Beet Marmalade

Preparation Time: 5 Minutes | Cooking Time: 1 Hour | Servings: 4

Ingredients:

- 1/2 lbs. fresh beets
- 1 tbsp. canola oil
- 1 sliced lemon
- 1 cup sugar
- 1 cup packed brown sugar

- 1/3 cup maple syrup
- 2 tbsps. chopped crystallized ginger
- 1/8 tsp. salt
- 1 cinnamon stick
- 8 whole cloves

Directions:

1. Preheat oven to 400°F.
2. Peel beets and cut into wedges. Place in a baking pan; drizzle with canola oil and toss to coat. Roast 5060 minutes or until tender. Cool slightly.
3. Put the cinnamon stick and cloves in a cheesecloth.
4. Pulse beets in a food processor until finely chopped. Transfer to a saucepan.
5. Add sugars, sliced lemon, maple syrup, ginger, salt, and spice bag. Bring to a boil, then simmer, uncovered, 1 hour to 1 hour 15 minutes until thickened.
6. Remove from heat, discard spice bag, and let cool slightly.
7. Fill 1cup containers to within 1/2 inch of tops. Cover with lids.

Grapefruit-Lemon Marmalade

Preparation Time: 5 Minutes | Cooking Time: 60 Minutes | Servings: 4

Ingredients:

- 3 clean grapefruits
- 2 clean medium lemons
- 4 cup water
- 5 cup sugar, granulated

Directions:

1. Cut the grapefruits and lemons into quarters, then slice thinly. Place the fruits and water in a large, heavy bottomed pot or saucepan. Bring to a boil and cook for about 30 minutes, or until rind is tender.
2. Reduce heat and add the sugar, stirring constantly, until the sugar is dissolved completely. Add ginger and increase heat, cook until it reaches setting point 220 F.
3. Transfer marmalade to hot sterilized jars, leaving 1/4-inch headspace. Cover tightly with lid.
4. Place jars in a hot water bath. Process for 10 minutes. Cool completely at room temperature.
5. Store in a cool, dark place. Keep refrigerated once opened.

Cherry Marmalade

Preparation Time: 5 Minutes | Cooking Time: 60 Minutes | Servings: 4

Ingredients:

- 4 tbsps. lime
- 4 cup cherries
- 2/3 cup peeled and chopped orange
- 3-1/2 cup sugar

Directions:

1. Take a large pan and mix cherries, orange and juice in it. Make them boil at medium heat. Low the flame and add cove with gentle boiling with frequent stirring for 20 minutes. Keep boiling with slow stirring.
2. Now boil hard with frequent stirring as the mixture gets gel like, for about 30 minutes. Remove the flame.
3. Pour the hot marmalade into sterilized jars. Remove the air bubble by adding more marmalade. Seal them with lids.

Strawberry Lemon Marmalade

Preparation Time: 5 Minutes | Cooking Time: 60 Minutes | Servings: 4

Ingredients:

- 6 cup sugar
- 1 tbsp. lime
- 1/4 cup peeled and sliced lemons
- 6 tbsps. classic pectin
- 4 cup crushed strawberries

Directions:

1. Get the canners prepared. Heat jars with simmering water. Don't boil them. Wash the lids with hot soapy water.
2. Mix the lemon peels with water in a pan. Cover the pan. Boil the mixture at medium flame and let them boil for about 5 minutes, until the peel gets softened. Drain the liquid.
3. Now include the lime and strawberries to lemon peel and mix them. Slowly stir the pectin. Heat the mixture at high flame with occasional stirring.
4. Include sugar and stir until it dissolves. Make the mixture to get boiled for one minute with constant stirring. Remove the flame and skim off the foam if required.
5. Pour the jam into sterilized jars with ladle. Cover them with lids and seal them.
6. Process the jars in boiled water canner for about 10 minutes. Remove the jars and allows them to cool.

Three-Citrus Marmalade

Preparation Time: 5 Minutes | Cooking Time: 60 Minutes | Servings: 4

Ingredients:

- 3 large lemons
- 6 cup sugar
- 4 medium navel oranges
- 2 pink grapefruit
- 4 cup poached zest liquid

Directions:

1. Wash the fruit thoroughly and let them dry. Use the peeler to remove the zest of fruit. Cut the zest into strips by using fine confetti. Mix the zest in the pot along with 6 cups of water. Make them boil at reduced flame and allow them to simmer for 30 minutes.
2. As the zest cooks, cut the white pith off the fruit and separate their membranes.
3. Drain the zest and save the liquid or cooking.
4. Take a large stainless-steel pot, add zest in it with citrus fruit, 6 cups of sugar, 4 cups of liquid from the zest, and cheesecloth roll. Boil them and cook instantly as the mixture gets heated to 220 degrees.
5. Stir them before removing the flame for helping the zest to become spread evenly throughout the marmalade.
6. Pour out hot marmalade into the sterilized jars. Remove the air bubble and cover them with lids.
7. Process the jars in boiled water canner for about 10 minutes. Allow them to cool.

Healthy Peach Preserves

Preparation Time: 5 Minutes | Cooking Time: 60 Minutes | Servings: 4

Ingredients:

- 12 crisp peaches, hollowed and sliced
- 4 1/2 cups white sugar
- 1 (2 ounce) bundle dry pectin

Directions:

1. Crush 1 cup slashed peaches in the base of a heavypot. Include remaining peaches, and set skillet over medium-low warmth. Convey to a low boil, and cook for around 20 minutes or until peaches get to be fluid (my family loves a couple of bits of peach left).

2. Empty peaches into a dish, and after that measure 6 cups once again into the cup. Include sugar, and heat to the point of boiling over medium warmth. Continuously blend in dry pectin, and boil for 1 minute.
3. Expel from warmth following 1 moment, and exchange to disinfected cups. Process in high temp water shower canner for 10 minutes. Let cool, and place on rack.

Healthy Watermelon Preserves

Preparation Time: 5 Minutes | Cooking Time: 60 Minutes | Servings: 4

Ingredients:

- 2 pounds watermelon
- 3 cups white sugar
- 3 lemons - flushed, cut and seeded

Directions:

1. Evacuate the green skin of the melon, and craps the white part into little shapes, leaving the red tissue for the most part in place. Expel seeds.
2. In a heavy stockpot, join 4 cups of the readied watermelon, sugar and lemons. Heat to the point of boiling over medium warmth, and let

the blend boil gradually for 2 hours, mixing once in a while. The temperature of the blend ought to be at 220 degrees F (105 degrees C) so the jam will set.
3. Sanitize the jugs and tops in boiling water for no less than 5 minutes. Pack the jam into the hot, sanitized cups, filling the jugs to inside 1/4 inch of the top. Run a blade or a slim spatula around the internal parts of the jugs after they have been filled to expel any air boils. Wipe the edges of the cups with a clammy paper towel to expel any food deposit. Top with covers, and screw on rings.
4. Place a rack in the base of a heavystockpot and fill most of the way with water. Heat to the point of boiling over high warmth, then painstakingly bring down the cups into the pot utilizing a holder. Leave a 2 inch space between the cups. Pour in all the more boiling water if important until the water level is no less than 1 inch over the highest points of the cups. Convey the water to a full boil, cover the pot, and process for 10 minutes.

Orange Marmalade

Preparation Time: 20 minutes | Cooking Time: 30 minutes | Servings: 4 pints

Ingredients:

- 2 large lemons
- 5 cup sugar
- 4 medium oranges
- 1-1/2 c. water
- 1/8 tsp. baking soda
- 13 oz. pectin
- 1/2 tsp. butter

Directions:

1. Heat the jars in the boiled water to sterilize them. Wash the lids with warm water too.
2. Peel off the lemons and oranges. Slice them thin and put in baking soda with water in a pan. Cook for 20 minutes and cover the pan. Remove the fruit pulp, get the fruit chopped and save the juice. Include the fruit and juice to mixture and simmer it for 10 minutes. Cover it.
3. Mix the fruit with lime and sugar in a saucepan. Add butter or margarine for foaming, if required.

Heat the mixture over high flame with frequent stirring.

4. Include pectin, instantly after squeezing the mixture from the pouch. Continue boiling for 1 minute, with continuous stirring. Remove from heat and skim the foam
5. Ladle the jam in sterilized jars. Cover the lids tightly.
6. Process them with boiling water Directions for 10 minutes.

Tangerine Marmalade

Preparation Time: 20 minutes | Cooking Time: 20 minutes | Servings: 4 pints

Ingredients:

- 1/2 tsp. vanilla extract
- 5-1/2 cup sugar
- 12 oz. tangerines
- 3 lbs. kumquats
- 1/2 cup vanilla bean

Directions:

1. Cut the fruits from the half and remove the flesh and skin. Cut them into thin slices. This will make 2 cups of the kumquat rinds.
2. Use fine mesh peeler to remove the zest of tangerines, be careful about the thin skin of tangerines.
3. Cut the peel of tangerines and divide the fruit into two. Put the segments of tangerine in a bowl. Collect the pulp of fruit in a separate bowl.
4. Mix the slices of kumquat with its juice, zests of tangerine, pulp of tangerines, sugar and water. Boil them, reduce the heat from medium to low and cook the mixture for about 15 minutes. Remove the flame.
5. Take a large pot containing water and boil it. Put the jars in it along with lids. Pour the hot jam into these sterilized jars. Cover them with lids tightly and allow them to get cooled.

Chapter 6: Chutneys & Relishes

Tasty Onion and Pepper Relish

Preparation Time: 15 Minutes | Cooking Time: 5 Hours and 10 Minutes | Servings: 7

Ingredients:

- 3 Onions, Large in Size and Sliced Thinly
- 8 Bell Peppers, Green in Color and Sliced into Thin Strips
- 3 Jalapeno Peppers, Seeded and Minced
- 6 Tablespoons of Spice, Pickled Variety
- 2 Cups of Sugar, White
- 1 teaspoon of Salt, For Taste
- 2 Cups of Vinegar, Apple Cider Variety

Directions::

1. The first thing that you want to do is place all of your ingredients into a large sized saucepan.
2. Bring this mixture to a boil over high heat. Once your mixture is boiling reduce the heat to low and allow to simmer for the next 5 minutes, making sure that you stir occasionally.
3. Remove from heat and allow to cool completely.
4. Pour your mixture into your canning jars and seal with your lids.
5. Boil your jars in some boiling water for the next 10 minutes. Remove and allow to cool slightly before placing into your fridge. Use whenever you are ready.

Rummage Style Relish

Preparation Time: 5 Minutes | Cooking Time: 13 Hours and 25 Minutes | Servings: 35

Ingredients:

- 8 Cups of Green Tomatoes, Cored and Finely Chopped
- 4 Cups of Red Tomatoes, Peeled, Cored and Finely Chopped
- 4 Cups of Cabbage, Roughly Chopped
- 3 Cups of Onion, Finely Sliced
- 2 Cups of Cucumber, Fresh and Finely Chopped
- 1 Cup of Bell Pepper, Green in Color and Finely Chopped
- 1 Cup of Bell Pepper, Red in Color and Finely Chopped
- 1/2 Cup of Salt, For Taste
- 4 Cups of Brown Sugar, Light and Packed
- 1 tablespoon of Celery Seed
- 1 tablespoon of Cinnamon, Ground Variety
- 1 tablespoon of Mustard Seed
- 1 teaspoon of Ginger, Ground Variety
- 2 Cloves of Garlic, Minced
- 1/2 teaspoons of Cloves, Ground Variety
- 2 Quarts of Vinegar

Directions::

1. First use a large sized bowl and mix together your first 7 ingredients until thoroughly combined. Season with your salt and allow to sit for the next 12 to 14 hours. After this time drain and rinse under some running water.
2. Then use a large sized pot and mix together your remaining ingredients until thoroughly combined.
3. Set over medium heat and bring your mixture to a boil, stirring thoroughly to dissolve your sugar.
4. Allow to simmer for the next 10 minutes before adding in your vegetable.
5. Continue to simmer for the next 30 minutes. Remove from heat and allow to cool completely.
6. Pour your mixture into your canning jars and seal with your lids.
7. Boil your jars in some boiling water for the next 10 minutes. Remove and allow to cool slightly before placing into your fridge. Use whenever you are ready.

Corn Relish

Preparation Time: 15 Minutes | Cooking Time: 20 minutes | Servings: 2

Ingredients:

- Corn, cooked – 2 cups
- Peppers – 1/2 cup
- Onion – 1
- Garlic – 2 cloves
- Vinegar – 2/3 cup
- Sugar – 2 tbsp
- Salt – 2 tbsp
- Spices of your choice

Direction:

1. Combine corn with chopped vegetables, vinegar, sugar, and salt.
2. Bring to a boil and then simmer for 7 minutes.
3. Cool and refrigerate.

Cauliflower Zucchini Preserve

Preparation Time: 5 Minutes | Cooking Time: 2.5 hours (including wait time) | Servings: 4

Ingredients:

- Cauliflowers – 2 heads
- Zucchini – 1 cup
- Onions – 3
- Mustard seeds – 1 tbsp
- Turmeric – 1 tsp
- Vinegar – 4 cups
- Sugar – 2 cups

- Salt

Direction:

1. Wash and cut cauliflowers, zucchini, and onions.
2. Combine with salt and cover with ice.
3. Let it stand for two hours in the refrigerator, adding ice when necessary.
4. Combine remaining ingredients and bring to a boil.
5. Pack vegetables in jars and pour hot liquid into it.
6. Process in boilingwater canner for 10 minutes.

Cucumber Relish

Preparation Time: 15 Minutes | Cooking Time: 4 hours and 20 minutes | Servings: 5

Ingredients:

- 4 unpeeled and diced cucumbers
- 2 diced green peppers
- 1 diced red pepper
- 1 tablespoon of celery seed
- 3 cups of ground onions
- 3 cups of finely diced celery
- 1/4 cup of salt
- 2 cups of white vinegar
- 1 tablespoon of mustard seeds
- 3 1/2 cups of sugar

Directions

1. Place all the ingredients in a food processor and pulse until the cucumber are finely chopped.
2. Place the relish in a large bowl and cover with cold water, letting it sit for about 4 hours.
3. Drain the mixture and combine with sugar. Bring to a boil. As it heats up, liquids will come out. Stir until the sugar is dissolved.
4. Pack into jars, and let sit in bath for about 10 minutes.
5. Let cool completely before storing.

Rhubarb Chutney

Preparation Time: 5 Minutes | Cooking Time: 10 Minutes | Servings: 4

Ingredients:

- 8 cups sliced rhubarb
- 6 cups sliced onion
- 2 cups raisins
- 7 cups light brown sugar
- 4 cups apple cider vinegar
- 2 tbsps. salt
- 2 tsps. cinnamon
- 2 tsps. ginger
- 1 tsp. ground cloves
- 1/8 tsp. cayenne pepper

Directions:

1. Mix all the components together in a large pot.
2. Boil, then simmer gently until the liquid is slightly thickened.
3. Pour into sterile jars and wipe the rims.
4. Tighten the lids and process in a hot water bath for 10 minutes.

Mango Chutney

Preparation Time: 15 Minutes | Cooking Time: 1 hours | Servings: 4

Ingredients:

- 6 cups sliced green mangos
- 1/2 lb. fresh ginger
- 31/2 cups currants
- 8 cups sugar
- 2 cups vinegar
- 3 cups ground cayenne pepper
- 1 cup salt

Directions:

1. Peel the ginger and halve it.
2. Slice one half of the ginger into thin slices; chop the other half of the ginger roughly.
3. Grind the chopped ginger with half of the currants, using a blender or food processor, until well combined. Place all in a saucepan, except the mangoes.
4. Cook over medium heat for 15 minutes.
5. Meanwhile, to make 6 cups, cut, halve, pit, and slice the green mangos.
6. After 15 minutes of cooking, add the mangos and simmer for another 30 minutes or until the mangos are tender and the mixture has thickened.
7. Pour into shot glasses, clean the rims, and screw the lids and rings together.
8. Use the boiling water bath process: pints and quarts for 10 minutes in both.

Green Tomato Chutney

Preparation Time: 5 Minutes | Cooking Time: 15 Minutes | Servings: 4

Ingredients:

- 21/2 lbs. chopped green tomatoes
- 11/4 cups brown sugar, packed
- 1 cup chopped red onion
- 1 cup golden raisins
- 1 cup cider vinegar
- 2 tbsps. minced ginger
- 1 tbsp. mustard seeds
- 1 tsp. chili pepper flakes
- 1 tsp. fennel seeds
- 1 tsp. salt
- 1/2 tsp. ground allspice
- 1/8 tsp. ground cloves
- 1 cinnamon stick
- pinch of ground nutmeg

Directions:

1. Put all of the ingredients in a 4quart pot. Bring to a boil and then reduce to a simmer for 45 minutes while covered.
2. Spoon the chutney into sterilized jars, filling them to 1/4inch from the rim.
3. Rinse the rims clean and place lids on the jars.
4. Finish the processing in a boiling water bath for 15 minutes.

Plum Tomato Chutney

Preparation Time: 5 Minutes | Cooking Time: 10 Minutes | Servings: 4

Ingredients:

- 4 tomatoes, chopped
- 6 chopped plums
- 2 chopped green chilies
- 4 tbsps. grated ginger
- 1 tsp. lemon zest
- Juice of 1 lemon
- 2 bay leaves
- Pinch of salt
- 1/2 cup plus 2 tbsps. brown sugar
- 2 tsps. vinegar
- Pinch black pepper
- 4 tsps. Vegetable oil

Directions:

1. Heat the oil in a deep saucepan. Add the bay leaves, ginger, and green chilies, and stir. Add the tomatoes and plums. Add the salt, zest, lemon juice, and vinegar. Stir in the sugar and pepper, cover, and cook for 3 minutes.
2. Spoon the chutney into sterilized jars, leaving a 1/2inch headspace. Wipe the edge of the jar rim clean and add the lid. Process these in a boiling water bath for 10 minutes.

Fruit Chutney

Preparation Time: 15 Minutes | Cooking Time: hours | Servings: 4

Ingredients:

- 1 tbsp. canola oil
- 4 cups chopped onion
- 1 tbsp. minced garlic
- 8 cups prepared fresh fruits, peeled (including pears, peaches, tomatoes and apples)
- 1 cup mixed dried fruits, chopped
- 1 cup granulated sugar
- 1 cup white vinegar

- 1 cup water
- 1 tsp. crushed red pepper
- 1 tsp. salt

Directions:

1. In a sizable pan, heat the oil and cook the onion about 6 minutes. Add the garlic and stir for 30 seconds.
2. Stir in the fresh fruit, dried fruit, sugar, vinegar, water, red pepper flakes, and salt.
3. Boil while stirring often, then reduce the heat and simmer for 30 minutes.
4. Spoon the chutney into sterilized jars to within 1/2inch of the rim.
5. Rinse the rims clean and place the lids on each jar.
6. Can the jars in a water bath for 15 minutes.

Garlicky Lime Chutney

Preparation Time: 5 Minutes | Cooking Time: 60 Minutes | Servings: 4

Ingredients:

- 12 diced limes
- 12 sliced garlic cloves
- 1 sliced ginger
- 8 green chile peppers
- 1 tbsp. chili powder
- 1 cup distilled white vinegar
- 3/4cup sugar

Directions:

1. Prepare a hot water bath. Place the jars in it to keep warm. Wash the lids and rings in hot, soapy water, and set aside.
2. In a medium saucepan, combine the limes, garlic, ginger, chiles, and chili powder. Stir well, and bring to a simmer.
3. Stir in the sugar and vinegar, then simmer for 1 hour 10 minutes
4. Ladle the chutney into the prepared jars, leaving 1/4 inch of headspace.
5. Rinse the rims clean and seal with the lids and rings.
6. Process the jars in a hot water bath for 20 minutes.

Curried Apple Chutney

Preparation Time: 5 Minutes | Cooking Time: 15 Minutes | Servings: 4

Ingredients:

- 2 quarts apples, peeled, cored and chopped
- 2 pounds raisins
- 4 cups brown sugar
- 1 cup onion, chopped
- 1 cup sweet pepper, chopped
- 3 tbsps. mustard seed
- 2 tbsps. ground ginger
- 2 tsps. allspice
- 2 tsps. curry powder
- 2 tsps. salt
- 2 hot red peppers, chopped
- 1 clove garlic, minced
- 4 cups vinegar

Directions:

1. In a large saucepan, mix all of the ingredients together. Bring to a boil and simmer for 1 hour.
2. Spoon the chutney into sterilized jars, leaving a 1/2 inch headspace. Wipe the jars' edge rim clean and add the lid. Process jars in a water bath for 10 minutes.

Spicy Green Tomato Chutney

Preparation Time: 5 Minutes | Cooking Time: 60 Minutes | Servings: 4

Ingredients:

- 2-1/2 cups spiced cider vinegar
- 3 cups shallots, finely chopped
- 2 quarters small green tomatoes, peeled and thinly sliced
- 1 tsp. celery salt
- 4 cups finely chopped apples
- 2 sweet red or green peppers
- Dry, hot chilies (four to six depending on heat strength)
- 2-1/4 cups brown sugar
- 2 cups ripe tomatoes, peeled and chopped
- salt

Directions

1. Combine 2-1/2 cups of apple cider vinegar, 1 stick of cinnamon, 1 teaspoon of allspice, whole cloves, black peppercorns, and & frac12; teaspoon ground nutmeg in a medium ability boiling pot.
2. Bring the fire on, and nearly get it to the boil.
3. Remove from the heat immediately and allow to cool down to room temperature.
4. Strain before applying to the chutney.
5. Black tomatoes to be peeled:
6. Place bowl, pot, or kettle in heat-proof.
7. Pour over boiling water to cover, letting them rest for three minutes.
8. Pierce peel with a sharp knife's tip and pull off the skin.

9. Slice very thinly on those tomatoes.
10. Pour in a colander over a tub, or green tomato slices with salt in a sink plate.
11. Let them drain for two hours.

In the meantime:

1. Peel, chop the apples sweet, core, and finely to make 4 cups.
2. A place to ready for use in acidulated water.
3. Clean shallots, then finely chop them to make 3 cups.
4. Prepare sweet peppers by washing, seeding, halving, and de rib.
5. Place under broiler or over open flames until the skin is charred and fleece away. Remove peppers; slice them thinly.
6. Place the chilies in a bag with cheesecloth.
7. Rinse green tomatoes at the end of two hours.
8. Combine green tomato slices, spiced strained vinegar, shallots, apples, hot chili bag, brown sugar, and celery salt in a large bowl.
9. Bring to a boil, cook for 15 minutes or until most of the liquid has evaporated.
10. Remove broiled, ripe tomatoes, and sweet peppers.
11. Simmer for about an hour, until dark.
12. Remove the bag of chili.
13. Pour into shot glasses, clean the rims, screw the lids and rings together.
14. Boiling water bath process: pints and quarts 10 minutes in both.

Orange Cranberry Chutney

Preparation Time: 5 Minutes | Cooking Time: 60 Minutes | Servings: 4

Ingredients:

- White onion, chopped (2 cups)
- White vinegar, distilled, 5% (2 cups)
- Cinnamon sticks (3 pieces)
- Sugar, white (1-1/2 cups)
- Ginger, fresh, peeled, grated (4 teaspoons)
- Cranberries, fresh, whole (24 ounces)
- Raisins, golden (2 cups)
- Sugar, brown, packed (1-1/2 cups)
- Orange juice, bottled (1 cup)

Directions:

1. After thoroughly rinsing the cranberries, put in the Dutch oven (large). Add the remaining ingredients and toss to combine.
2. Heat over high heat and bring the mixture to boil. Once boiling, turn the heat down to medium-low and let the mixture simmer for fifteen minutes or until you're the cranberries are tenderized. Make sure to stir to avoid scorching frequently.
3. Once the chutney is done, discard the cinnamon sticks. Pour the chutney into clean and hot Mason jars (half-pint), making sure to leave half an inch of headspace in each.
4. Get rid of air bubbles in the jars before fitting their rims with the lids. Place in the pressure canner.
5. Process for ten minutes.

Apple and Cherry Chutney

Preparation Time: 15 Minutes | Cooking Time: 60 Minutes | Servings: 4

Ingredients:

- 1 apple, chopped
- 1 pound cherries, pitted
- 1/2 cup rice vinegar
- 1 cup cider vinegar
- 2 tablespoons minced ginger
- 1 large onion, chopped
- 1/4 cup brown sugar
- 1/4 cup white sugar
- 1/4 teaspoon ground nutmeg
- 2 tablespoons Chinese five-spice

- 1 teaspoon salt

Directions:

1. In a large pot, combine apple, onion, rice vinegar, apple cider vinegar, cherries, nutmeg, five-spice powder, ginger, sugars, and salt; bring a gentle simmer and lower heat low. Cook for about 1 hour, stirring occasionally. Remove from heat and let cool. Chill before serving. Preserve in an airtight container in the fridge for up to four weeks.

Apple Thyme Chutney

Preparation Time: 10 Minutes | Cooking Time: 20 Minutes | Servings: 2

Ingredients:

- 3 peeled and cored large apples, chopped
- 2 oz. white sugar
- 1 oz. Apple cider vinegar
- 1/2 oz. ground thyme
- 1 bay leaf and salt to taste
- 1 oz. apple brandy

Directions:

2. Mix all ingredients except for brandy and salt in a medium saucepan on medium-low heat. Partially cover the pan and simmer the mixture for 1 hour until thick and sticky.
3. Add brandy 5-10 minutes before the end of the cooking time and stir well. Season with salt.
4. Put the chutney into hot, prepared jars and seal according to canners' instructions. Cool and

place in the refrigerator before use. Remove bay leaf before using.

Cantaloupe Chutney

Preparation Time: 20 Minutes | Cooking Time: 100 Minutes | Servings: 5

Ingredients:

- 3 Medium cantaloupes
- 1 pound of dried apricots
- 1 fresh hot chili
- 2 cups of raisins
- 1 tsp. ground cloves
- 1 tsp. ground nutmeg
- 2 tbsp. salt
- 2 tbsp. mustard seed
- 1/4 cup fresh ginger, chopped
- 3 cloves garlic
- 41/2 cups apple cider vinegar
- 21/4 cups brown sugar
- 4 onions
- 1/2 cup orange juice
- 2 tbsp. orange zest

Directions:

1. Thinly slice the apricots and put them into a large bowl.
2. Chop the ginger and garlic thinly and add to the dish.
3. Stir in the chili, seeded and diced, after adding to the pot.

4. Add raisins, cloves, cinnamon, nutmeg, and mustard seeds.
5. Mix and set aside.
6. Mix the sugar and vinegar in a non-reactive pot or kettle and boil over medium heat.
7. Add mixture to the pot in a bowl and return to a moderate simmer.
8. Keep simmering for 45 minutes.
9. Meanwhile, chop the onions and place them in a bowl.
10. Peel and seed the cantaloupe.
11. Split the fruit into cubes of 1/2 an inch.
12. Add onions.
13. In the cup, add orange juice and zest; mix well.
14. Once the vinegar mixture has finished 45 minutes of cooking time, add the cantaloupe mixture to the bowl, bring it back to a simmer, and start cooking for another 45 minutes or until thickened.
15. Pour into shot glasses, clean the rims, and screw the lids and rings together.
16. Boiling water bath process: pints and quarts are 10 minutes each.

Coconut Chutney

Preparation Time: 15 Minutes | Cooking Time:0 | Servings: 1

Ingredients:

- 1/4 teaspoon cumin seeds
- 1/2 teaspoon mustard seed
- 3 peppers fresh red chili peppers, chopped
- 1 tablespoon vegetable oil
- 1/2 cup plain yogurt
- 1/2 fresh whole coconut, grated

Directions:

1. Process together yogurt and coconut to a fine paste; transfer to a bowl.
2. Heat oil in a saucepan and stir in cumin seeds, mustard seeds, and chili pepper; cook until the seeds start popping; add the seed mixture into the coconut mixture and stir to combine well. Cover and refrigerate until ready to serve.

Delicious Bourbon Bacon Chutney

Preparation Time: 10 Minutes | Cooking Time: 45 Minutes | Servings: 4

Ingredients:

- 1/2 cup bourbon
- 12 slices bacon, chopped
- 3 cloves garlic, minced
- 2 tablespoons butter
- 2 medium red onions, chopped

Directions:

1. Heat a skillet over medium heat; add in bacon and cook for about 10 minutes or until golden; lower the heat and add in butter, garlic and onions. Cook for about 20 minutes or until onions is tender. Pour in bourbon and simmer for about 15 minutes or until the liquid evaporates.
2. Serve and store the rest in jars in the fridge.

Fresh Ginger Apple and Cranberry Chutney

Preparation Time: 10 Minutes | Cooking Time: 10 Minutes | Servings: 4

Ingredients:

- 1 cup raisins
- 1/4 teaspoon ground cloves
- 4 cups cranberries
- 1 teaspoon fresh ginger, minced
- 2 teaspoons cinnamon
- 3/4 cup packed brown sugar
- 1/2 cup white sugar
- 1 cup water
- 1/2 cup chopped celery
- 1/2 cup chopped apple
- 1/2 cup minced onion

Directions:

1. In a saucepan, combine water, sugars, raisins, cranberries, cinnamon, cloves, and ginger; bring to a boil and simmer for about 5 minutes. Stir in celery, apples, and onion and cook for about 10 minutes or until thick. Let cool and transfer to containers. Store in the fridge.

Green Mango Chutney

Preparation Time: 15 Minutes | Cooking Time: 30 Minutes | Servings: 3

Ingredients:

- 32 oz. unripe diced green mango
- 4 oz. raisins
- 2 oz. finely chopped serrano peppers

- 6 minced cloves garlic
- 3/4 oz. Fresh ginger root, minced
- 1/4 oz. Lemon zest
- 1/2 oz. black pepper
- 1 oz. molasses
- 1 small cinnamon stick
- 4 whole cloves
- 8 oz. water
- 8 oz. cider vinegar

Directions:

1. Mix the ingredients and simmer for 30 minutes until the mixture reaches a jam-like consistency.
2. Stir often. Once the correct consistency has been achieved, remove from the fire and left to cool.
3. Store chutney in the refrigerator in glass jars or the freezer in plastic containers.

Asparagus - Spears

Preparation Time: 20 minutes | Cooking Time: 30 minutes | Servings: 9 pints

Ingredients:

- 16 pounds asparagus spears
- 10 tbsps. salt
- Boiling water

Directions

1. In a large pot, cover the asparagus with the boiling water and add the salt. Boil for 3 minutes. Fill sterilized jars loosely with the asparagus and liquid, leaving a 1-inch headspace.
2. Adjust the jar lids and process the jars for 30 minutes in a pressure canner at 10 pounds of pressure for a pressure canner with a weighted gauge or 11 pounds if the pressure canner has a dial gauge.

Lima Beans - Shelled

Preparation Time: 20 minutes | Cooking Time: 50 minutes | Servings: 9 pints

Ingredients:

- 18 pounds lima beans, shelled
- 10 tablespoons salt
- Boiling water

Directions

1. In a large pot, cover the beans with the boiling water and add the salt. Boil the beans for 10 minutes. Fill sterilized jars loosely with beans and liquid, leaving a 1-inch headspace.
2. Adjust the jar lids and process the jars for 40 minutes in a pressure canner at 10 pounds of pressure for a pressure canner with a weighted gauge or 11 pounds if the pressure canner has a dial gauge.

White Potatoes - Cubed or Whole

Preparation Time: 20 minutes | Cooking Time: 45 minutes | Servings: 9 pints

Ingredients:

- 13 pounds potatoes
- 4 tbsps. salt
- Boiling water

Directions

1. Wash and peel the potatoes and place them in ascorbic acid solution, made up of 1 gallon of water with 1 cup of lemon juice to prevent them from darkening. Drain the potatoes and allow to cook for 10 minutes in boiling salt

water. You may use paper towels to drain them.

2. Fill sterilized jars with the potatoes. Cover the potatoes with fresh boiling water, leaving a 1-inch headspace.
3. Process in a pressure canner for 35 minutes at 10 pounds of pressure for a pressure canner with a weighted gauge or 11 pounds if the pressure canner has a dial gauge.

Italian Style Stewed Tomatoes

Preparation Time: 20 minutes | Cooking Time: 25 minutes | Servings: 6 pints

Ingredients:

- 4 quarts chopped tomatoes
- 1 cup chopped onions
- 1/2 cup chopped green peppers
- 4 garlic cloves, minced
- 3 tsps. dry basil
- 1 tsp. dry oregano
- 4 tsps. sugar
- 1 tsp. salt
- 1 tsp. black pepper

Directions

1. Place all of the ingredients in a large saucepan and bring to a boil. Let this mixture simmer for about 10 minutes, stirring occasionally.
2. Pack sterilized jars with the hot tomato mixture, leaving a 1/2-inch head space. Remove any air bubbles, clean the rims and adjust lids.
3. Process the jars for 15 minutes in a pressure canner at 10 pounds of pressure for a pressure canner with a weighted gauge or 11 pounds if the pressure canner has a dial gauge.

Tomatoes - Whole

Preparation Time: 20 minutes | Cooking Time: 45 minutes | Servings: 7-quart pints

Ingredients:

- 21 pounds whole tomatoes, skinned
- 4 tbsps. salt
- 3/4 cup lemon juice, optional
- Boiling water

Directions

1. Place the tomatoes and the salt in a saucepan and cover with the water. Bring to a boil and cook for 5 minutes.
2. Pack sterilized jars with the tomatoes and the hot liquid, leaving a 1/2-inch head space. Remove any air bubbles, clean the rim and adjust lids.
3. If omitting the lemon juice, process the jars for 45 minutes in a pressure canner at 10 pounds of pressure for a pressure canner with a weighted gauge or 11 pounds if the pressure canner has a dial gauge.
4. If using lemon juice, process the jars for 10 minutes in a boiling water bath.

Spiced Beets

Preparation Time: 20 minutes | Cooking Time: 25 minutes | Servings: 2 half pints

Ingredients:

- 1/4 tsp. salt

- 3/4 tsp. allspice
- 3/4 tsp. cloves
- 1/4 stick cinnamon
- 1/4-piece mace
- 1-1/2 tsps. celery seed
- 2 cups cider vinegar, 5% acidity
- 1 cup sugar
- 2 pints beets

Directions

1. Tie the salt and the spices in a thin cloth bag. Boil the vinegar, sugar, and spices for 15 minutes. Sterilize a quart jar for 15 minutes. Remove the jar from the water and pour in the vinegar mix. Fix the lid and set aside for 2 weeks.
2. Remove the spice bag. Cook fresh beets until tender but firm, and let cool. Peel the beets. Heat the vinegar and add 1/2 cup of the beet liquid. Add the beets and simmer for 15 minutes.
3. Pack into sterile jars, being sure the vinegar covers the beets. Remove air bubbles and adjust the lids. Process for 10 minutes in a boiling water bath.

Spicy Carrots

Preparation Time: 20 minutes | Cooking Time: 30 minutes | Servings: 2 half pints

Ingredients:

- 1/4 tsp. salt
- 3/4 tsp. allspice
- 3/4 tsp. cloves
- 1/4 stick cinnamon
- 1/4-piece mace
- 1-1/2 tsps. celery seed
- 2 cups cider vinegar, 5% acidity
- 1 cup sugar
- 2 pints carrots

Directions

1. Tie the salt and the spices in thin cloth bag. Boil the vinegar, sugar, and spices for 15 minutes. Sterilize a quart jar for about 15 minutes in boiling water. Remove the jar from the water and pour in the vinegar mix. Fix the lid and set aside for 2 weeks.
2. Remove the spice bag. Cook fresh carrots until tender but firm and let cool. Heat the vinegar and add 1/2 cup of the carrot liquid. Add the carrots and simmer for 15 minutes.
3. Pack into sterile jars, being sure the vinegar covers the carrots. Remove air bubbles and adjust the lids. Process 10 minutes in a boiling water bath.

Chapter 7: Salsas & Sauces

Classic Fiesta Salsa

Preparation Time: 15 Minutes | Cooking Time: 2 hours | Servings: 32

Ingredients:

- 4 1/2 Cups of Tomatoes, Fresh and Finely Diced
- 3 Tablespoons of Vinegar, White
- 1/4 Cup of Salsa, Your Favorite Kind
- 2, 16 Ounces of Canning Jars, With Lids and Rings

Directions:

1. The first thing that you will want to do is combine your diced tomatoes, vinegar and favorite kind of salsa in a large sized saucepan placed over medium heat.
2. Cook your mixture until boiling. Once your mixture is boiling reduce the heat to low and allow to simmer for the next 5 minutes.
3. Remove from heat and allow to cool completely.
4. Pour your mixture into your canning jars and seal with your lids.
5. Boil your jars in some boiling water for the next 10 minutes. Remove and allow to cool slightly before placing into your fridge. Use whenever you are ready.

Chipotle Style Plum Sauce

Preparation Time: 5 Minutes | Cooking Time: 4 Hours and 40 Minutes | Servings: 124

Ingredients:

- 5 Quarts of Plums, Ripe and Pitted
- 4 Cloves of Garlic, Pressed
- Onion, Finely Diced
- 6 Cups of Sugar, White
- 1/2 Cup of Vinegar, Apple Cider Variety
- Tablespoons of Chipotle Seasoning, Southwest Variety
- 1 tablespoon of Garlic Seasoning, Roasted Variety
- 1 Jalapeno Pepper, Finely Diced
- 7 teaspoons of Salt, For Taste
- 1 teaspoon of Smoke Flavoring, Liquid Variety
- 8 Canning Jars, With Lids and Rings

Directions::

1. First place your plums into a colander set inside of a large sized bowl and squeeze to force the juices out. Repeat until all of your plums have been juiced.
2. Pour this juice along with your garlic and onion into a medium sized saucepan and place over medium heat. Bring this mixture to a boil before reducing the heat to low. Continue to simmer until your onions turns translucent.
3. Then pour this mixture into a large sized pot and add in your remaining ingredients. Stir thoroughly until your salt and sugar fully dissolve. Bring this mixture to a boil over medium heat. Once boiling reduce the heat to low and cook until your mixture is thick in consistency. This should take about 1 1/2 hours.
4. After this time remove from heat and allow to cool completely.
5. Pour your mixture into your canning jars and seal with your lids.
6. Boil your jars in some boiling water for the next 10 minutes. Remove and allow to cool slightly

before placing into your fridge. Use whenever you are ready.

Harvest Time Tomato Marinara Sauce

Preparation Time: 15 Minutes | Cooking Time: 5 hours | Servings: 45

Ingredients:

- 25 Pounds of Tomatoes, Plum Variety, Cored and Cut in Halves
- 3 Bay Leaves, Fresh
- 1/2 Tablespoons of Honey, Raw
- 1 tablespoon of Oregano, Dried
- 1 tablespoon of Salt, For Taste
- teaspoons of Black Pepper, Ground
- 1/2 Cup of Olive Oil, Extra Virgin Variety
- 1 Pound of Onions, Yellow in Color and Finely Chopped
- 10 Cloves of Garlic, Minced
- 10, 1 Quart Canning Jars, With Lids and Rings
- 10 teaspoons of Salt, For Taste and Evenly Divided
- 1 3/4Cups of Lemon Juice, Fresh and Evenly Divided

Directions::

1. First place your first 6 ingredients into a large sized saucepan. Cover with some water and stir thoroughly to combine.
2. Cover and bring this mixture to a boil over medium to high heat.
3. Once boiling reduce the heat to low and allow to simmer for the next 20 minutes uncovered, making sure to stir thoroughly. After this time

remove your bay leaves and season to your taste.

4. Next heat up your olive oil in a large sized skillet placed over medium to high heat. Once your oil is hot enough add in your onions and garlic and cook until your onions are soft to the touch. This should take about 10 minutes.
5. Next puree your tomatoes until smooth in consistency and add back to your saucepan. Add in your cooked garlic and onions and cook while uncovered over medium to high heat until your sauce becomes thick in consistency. This should take about 1 to 1 1/2 hours.
6. Remove from heat and allow to cool completely.
7. Pour your mixture into your canning jars and seal with your lids.
8. Boil your jars in some boiling water for the next 10 minutes. Remove and allow to cool slightly before placing into your fridge. Use whenever you are ready.

Carolina Style BBQ Peppers

Preparation Time: 5 Minutes | Cooking Time: 20 Minutes | Servings: 64

Ingredients:

- 2 Cups of Oil, Corn Variety
- 2 Cups of Vinegar, Cider Variety
- 2 Cups of Sugar, White
- 4 Cups of Ketchup, Your Favorite Kind
- Pound of Jalapeno Peppers, Fresh and Sliced into Thin Rings
- Dash of Oregano, Dried

- 1 Clove of Garlic, Minced

Directions::

1. First use a large sized pot and add in your first 4 ingredients and stir thoroughly until your sugar is fully dissolved.
2. Bring this mixture to a boil. Once your mixture is boiling add in your jalapeno peppers. Stir to combine.
3. Reduce your heat to low and allow your mixture to simmer for the next 10 minutes before seasoning with a dash of garlic and oregano. Remove from heat and allow to cool completely.
4. Pour your mixture into your canning jars and seal with your lids.
5. Boil your jars in some boiling water for the next 10 minutes. Remove and allow to cool slightly before placing into your fridge. Use whenever you are ready.

Tomato Salsa

Preparation Time: 15 Minutes | Cooking Time: 90 minutes | Servings: 6

Ingredients:

- Tomatoes – 12 cups
- Onions – 2 cups
- Cucumbers – 1 cup
- Peppers (green/red/jalapeno) – 3
- Garlic – 2 tbsp
- Sugar – 4 tbsp
- Salt – 2 tsp
- Vinegar – 1 1/2 cups

Direction:

1. Chop the vegetables.
2. Combine all the ingredients in a pot and boil for 45 minutes. It should reduce by half and thicken.
3. Pour into prepared jars and process in boilingwater canner for 20 minutes.

Thai Dipping Sauce

Preparation Time: 5 Minutes | Cooking Time: 40 Minutes | Servings: 4

Ingredients:

- Vinegar – 4 cups
- Sugar – 4 cups
- Red pepper flakes – 1/2 cup
- Salt – 1 tbsp

Direction:

1. Heat vinegar. Add sugar to it and boil until it dissolves.
2. Add garlic, pepper flakes, salt.
3. Boil for 2 minutes.
4. Ladle into prepared jars and process in boilingwater canner for 15 minutes.

Barbecue Sauce

Preparation Time: 15 Minutes | Cooking Time: 2 hours | Servings: 5

Ingredients:

- Onions – 3
- Garlic – 5 cloves
- Oil – 1 tbsp
- Tomato sauce – 6 cups
- Vinegar – 1 1/2 cups
- Chili powder – 4 tbsp
- Paprika – 2 tsp
- Honey – 1/2 cup
- Salt

Direction:

1. Saute the onions and garlic in oil.
2. Add all the other ingredients and bring to a boil.
3. Simmer for 45 minutes.
4. Transfer into jars.
5. Process in boilingwater canner for 20 minutes.

Zesty Salsa

Preparation Time: 5 Minutes | Cooking Time: 10 Minutes | Servings: 4

Ingredients:

- 10 cups of chopped tomatoes
- 5 cups of chopped and seeded bell peppers
- 5 cups of chopped onions
- 2 1/2 cups of hot peppers, chopped and seeded
- 1/4 cup of cider vinegar
- minced garlic cloves
- tablespoons of minced cilantro
- teaspoons of salt
- 1 can of tomato paste, about six ounces

Directions

1. Put all ingredients except for the tomato paste into a large pot.
2. Let simmer for about three minutes or until thick.
3. Mix in the tomato paste.
4. Ladle the hot salsa into jars, leaving about 1/4" head space.
5. Let the jars sit in a water bath for about 15 minutes.
6. Let cool completely before storing.

Homemade Pizza Sauce

Preparation Time: 15 Minutes | Cooking Time: 80 minutes | Servings: 4

Ingredients:

- 25-28 red and ripe tomatoes, mediumsized
- 2 large yellow onions, peeled
- 4 large garlic cloves, peeled
- 3 tablespoons of olive oil
- 2 tablespoons of lemon juice
- teaspoon freshly ground black pepper
- 1 tablespoon of white sugar
- tablespoons of chopped parsley
- 1 tablespoon of oregano
- 1 tablespoon of dry basil
- 1 teaspoon of dry rosemary
- 1 teaspoon of celery seed
- teaspoons of kosher salt

Directions

1. Peel the tomatoes. Blanch them for two to three minutes in boiling water so that they are easier to peel. Puree them in a blender or food processor.
2. Mince the onions and garlic cloves.
3. Sauté the onions and garlic in a large saucepan with the olive oil for about 34 minutes until tender and fragrant.
4. Add the tomato puree. Bring to a boil on mediumhigh heat. Reduce heat to low, and let simmer for 45 minutes
5. Once the sauce thickens, put it into jars
6. Let the jars sit in a water bath for about 25 minutes.
7. Let cool completely before storing.

Unripe Tomato Salsa

Preparation Time: 5 Minutes | Cooking Time: 60 Minutes | Servings: 4

Ingredients:

- 5 pounds of unpeeled green tomatoes, finely chopped
- 6 yellow onions, chopped small

- 3 jalapeños, chopped with the seeds
- 4 large green bell peppers, chopped
- 6 garlic cloves, minced
- cup of fresh cilantro, chopped
- 1 cup of lime juice
- 1 tablespoon of salt
- 1/2 tablespoon of cumin
- 1 tablespoon of dried oregano leaves
- tablespoons of pepper

Directions

1. Combine all of the ingredients together in a large pot and bring to a boil, mixing for the next 30 to 40 minutes.
2. After the time is up, and it's at a boil again, put the salsa into the sterilized jars. Let the jars sit in a water bath for about 15 minutes.
3. Let them sit at room temperature for about 24 hours before refrigerating or storing.

Applesauce

Preparation Time: 15 Minutes | Cooking Time: 20 minutes | Servings: 1

Ingredients:

- 3 pounds of cooking apples such as McIntosh, Cortland, Bramley
- 2 tablespoons white sugar (optional)
- 2 teaspoons of ground cinnamon (optional)
- Water

Directions

1. Peel, core, and then quarter the apples, put into large pot, cook until soft.
2. Puree the apples, and then put the mixture back into the pan and bring to a boil. Add sugar or cinnamon if desired.
3. Place into jars while boiling.
4. Let the jars sit in a water bath for about 20 minutes.
5. Let cool completely before storing.

Asian Plum Sauce

Preparation Time: 5 Minutes | Cooking Time: 60 Minutes | Servings: 4

Ingredients:

- 4 cloves of garlic, minced
- 1/4 cup of fresh ginger, grated
  - yellow onion, diced finely
- 1 cup of brown sugar
  - cups of water
- 1/8 cup of teriyaki sauce
- 1 teaspoon of sesame oil
- 1/8 cup of soy sauce
- 1/2 teaspoon of crushed and dried chili
- pounds of chopped and pitted plums
- 1 tablespoon of cornstarch
- 1 lemon, squeezed for the juice

Directions

1. Mix all of the ingredients together, and bring to a boil in a large pot for about 30 minutes.
2. Simmer for around 58 minutes or until it is thick, and then put into jars.
3. Let the jars sit in a water bath for about 10 minutes.
4. Let cool completely before storing. Store in a cool and dark place

Salsa Verde

Preparation Time: 15 Minutes | Cooking Time: 10 Minutes | Servings: 4

Ingredients:

- 3 glass pint jars with lids and bands
- 12 medium green tomatoes, cored, peeled and diced
- 6 to 8 jalapenos, seeded and minced
- 2 large red onions, diced
- teaspoon of minced garlic
- 1/2 cup of fresh lime juice
- 1/2 cup of fresh chopped cilantro
- 1 1/2 teaspoons ground cumin
- 1 teaspoon dried oregano
- Salt and pepper to taste

Directions:

1. Prepare your water bath canner as well as your lids and bands.
2. Combine the tomatoes, jalapenos, onion, garlic, and lime juice in a large saucepan.
3. Cover and bring to a boil then stir in the remaining ingredients.
4. Reduce heat and simmer for 5 minutes then spoon the mixture into your jars, leaving about 1/2inch of headspace.
5. Clean the rims add the lid and seal with a metal band then place the jars in the water bath canner and bring the water to boil.
6. Process the jars for 20 minutes then remove the jars and wipe them dry.
7. Place the jars on a canning rack and cool for 24 hours before storing it.

Simple Salsa

Preparation Time: 5 Minutes | Cooking Time: 10 Minutes | Servings: 4

Ingredients:

- 4 cups of slicing tomatoes (peeled, cored and chopped)
- 2 cups of green chilies (seeded and chopped)
- 3/4cup of onions (chopped)
- 1/2 cup of jalapeno peppers (seeded and chopped)
- 4 garlic cloves (chopped finely)
- teaspoon of ground cumin
- 1 tablespoon of cilantro
- 1 tablespoon of oregano
- cups of distilled white vinegar
- 1 1/2 teaspoon of table salt

Directions:

1. Place all the ingredients above in a large pot. Place the pot on the stove and bring to a rolling boil while stirring constantly to prevent burning.
2. Reduce the heat a bit and let the mixture simmer for about 20 minutes. Stir frequently.
3. Divide the salsa among 4 jars. Make sure to leave about 1/2inch of space at the top of each jar. Place the lids on the jars and process using the water bath canning Direction for 15 to 25 minutes.

Mango Salsa

Preparation time: 15 minutes | Cooking time: 10 minutes | Servings: 4

Ingredients:

- 1/4 cup of cider vinegar, 5%
- teaspoons of ginger, chopped finely
- 1 1/2 cup of red bell pepper, diced
- 1/2 teaspoon of red pepper flakes, crushed
- 6 cups of mango, unripe, diced
- 1/2 cup of yellow onion, chopped finely
- teaspoons of garlic, chopped finely
- 1 cup of brown sugar, light

Directions:

1) Thoroughly wash the mangoes and the rest of the produce.
2) Peel the mangoes before chopping in halfinch cubes.
3) Chop the yellow onion into fine bits and dice the red bell pepper in halfinch strips. Place in a stockpot or Dutch oven. Add all other ingredients, stir to combine, and heat over high heat.
4) Once the mixture is boiling, give it a good stir to dissolve the sugar. Turn the heat down to medium and allow the mixture to simmer for about five minutes.
5) Pour the hot salsa into clean and hot Mason jars, leaving half an inch of headspace in each jar. Pour the hot liquid into it to fill each jar half an inch from the rim.
6) Take out any air bubbles before securing the jar lids. Place in the pressure canner and process for ten minutes.

Green Salsa

Preparation time: 5 minutes | Cooking time: 10 minutes | Servings: 4

Ingredients:

- 7 Cups of chopped green tomatoes
- 3 Cups of chopped jalapenos
- 2 Cups of chopped red onions
- 2 Teaspoons of minced garlic
- 1/2 Cup of lime juice
- 1/2 Cup of finely packed chopped cilantro
- 2 Tsp. ground cumin

Directions:

1. Combine all the vegetables and the garlic and lime in a saucepan and boil then simmer for 5 minutes, spoon salsa into canning jars, and leave 1/4" at the top for the canning process.

Tomatillo Salsa

Preparation time: 15 minutes | Cooking time: 10 minutes | Servings: 5

Ingredients:

- 1/2 pounds tomatillos (about 12 medium), husked and rinsed
- 1 to 2 medium jalapeños, stemmed (omit for mild salsa, use 1 jalapeño for medium salsa and 2 jalapeños for hot salsa, and note that spiciness will depend on heat of actual peppers used)
- 1/2 cup chopped white onion (about 1/2 medium onion)

- 1/4 cup packed fresh cilantro leaves (more if you love cilantro)
- tablespoons to 1/4 cup lime juice (1 to 2 medium limes, juiced), to taste
- 1/2 to 1 teaspoon salt, to taste
- Optional variation: 1 to 2 diced avocados, for creamy avocado salsa verde

Directions:

1. Preheat the broiler with a rack about 4 inches below the heat source. Place the tomatillos and jalapeño(s) on a rimmed baking sheet and broil until they're blackened in spots, about 5 minutes.
2. Remove the baking sheet from the oven, carefully flip over the tomatillos and pepper(s) with tongs, and broil for 4 to 6 more minutes, until the tomatillos are splotchyblack and blistered.
3. Meanwhile, in a food processor or blender, combine the chopped onion, cilantro, 2 tablespoons lime juice and 1/2 teaspoon salt. Once the tomatillos are out of the oven, carefully transfer the hot tomatillos, pepper(s) and all of their juices into the food processor or blender.
4. Pulse until the mixture is mostly smooth and no big chunks of tomatillo remain, scraping down the sides as necessary, season to taste with additional lime juice and salt if desired.
5. The salsa will be thinner at first, but will thicken up after a few hours in the refrigerator, due to the naturally occurring pectin in the tomatillos. If you'd like to make creamy avocado salsa verde, let the salsa cool down before blending in 1 to 2 diced avocados (the more avocado, the creamier it gets).

Corn & Cherry Tomato Salsa

Preparation Time: 5 Minutes | Cooking Time: 10 Minutes | Servings: 4

Ingredients:

- 5 pounds cherry tomatoes, roughly chopped
- 2 cups corn kernels (about 2 large ears fresh, but frozenthawed is fine)
- cup red onion, finely chopped
- teaspoons salt
- 1/2 cup fresh lime juice (about 3 large or 4 medium limes)
- jalapeño peppers, seeded and minced
- 1 teaspoon chipotle chili powder, optional
- 1/2 cup chopped fresh cilantro

Directions:

1. Prepare the boiling water canner. Heat the jars in simmering water until they're ready for use. Do not boil. Wash the lids in warm soapy water and set them aside with the bands.
2. Bring all the ingredients to a boil in a large stainlesssteel or enameled saucepan. Reduce the heat and simmer for 5 to 10 minutes, stirring occasionally.
3. Ladle the hot salsa into a hot jar, leaving 1/2inch of headspace. Remove the air bubbles. Wipe the jar rim clean. Center the lid on the jar. Apply the band and adjust to fingertiptight.

Place the jar in the boiling water canner. Repeat until all the jars are filled.

4. Process the jars for 15 minutes, adjusting for altitude. Turn off the heat; remove the lid, and let the jars stand for 5 minutes. Remove the jars and let them cool.

Spicy Corn Salsa

Preparation Time: 15 Minutes | Cooking Time: 35 MINUTES | Servings: 5

Ingredients:

- 1/2 tsp chipotle chile powder
- 2 tsp ground cumin
- 4 tsp kosher salt
- 2 tbsp minced fresh garlic
- 1/4 cup sugar
- 1/4 cup chopped fresh cilantro
- 2 jalapeños, finely diced
- cup distilled white vinegar
- 1 cup diced poblanos
- 1 cup diced white onions
- cups tomatoes, peeled, seeded, cored, and diced
- cups corn kernels

Directions:

1. Combine all ingredients in a pot, bring to a boil, then reduce to a simmer for 15 minutes.
2. Ladle salsa into jars, leaving 1/2 inch headspace
3. Process jars for 15 minutes. Then, remove your jars and let cool for 24 hours before consumption or storage.

Black Beans and Corn Salsa

Preparation Time: 5 Minutes | Cooking Time: 60 Minutes | Servings: 4

Ingredients:

- 2 cups frozen corn
- 15 oz tomato sauce
- 12 oz tomato paste
- 1/3 cup vinegar
- 1/8 cup canning salt
- tsp black pepper
- 1 tsp cumin
- 6 garlic cloves, minced
- 1 cubanelle pepper, chopped
- 1 cup jalapeño pepper, chopped
- 1 1/2 cups green peppers
- 1/2 cups onion, chopped

Directions:

1. Into a large pot, mix everything, and bring to a slow boil for 10 minutes.
2. Then, ladle the salsa into jars.
3. Process for 10 minutes.
4. Remove jars, let cool for 12 hours.

Mago Pineapple Salsa

Preparation Time: 15 Minutes | Cooking Time: 2 hours | Servings: 5

Ingredients:

- 1/2 tsp salt
- 2 garlic cloves, minced
- tsp fresh ginger, grated
- 1/4 cup cider vinegar
- 1/4 lime juice
- 1/3 cup sugar
- 1/4 cup jalapeños, finely chopped
- 1 cup red sweet pepper
- 1 cup large sweet onion
- cups mangoes, peeled, chopped
- cups pineapple
- cups ripe tomatoes, cored, chopped

Directions:

1. Combine all ingredients in a large pot. Bring to a boil, then reduce to a simmer uncovered, for

10 minutes. Stirring occasionally. Then, remove from heat.

2. Ladle salsa into jars, with 1/2 inch headspace.
3. Process jars in boiling water for 20 minutes. Then, remove jars and let cool for 12 hours.

Chipotle Roasted Tomato Salsa

Preparation Time: 5 Minutes | Cooking Time: 60 Minutes | Servings: 8

Ingredients:

- 2 pounds tomatillos, husked
- 2 pounds plum tomatoes, diced
- 12 chipotle chili peppers, dried
- 12 cascabel chili peppers, dried
- garlic head, broken into pieces
- small onions, diced
- 1 cup distilled white vinegar
- 1 teaspoon table salt

Directions:

1. In a clean skillet, toast the chipotle and cascabel chilies until they become pliable. Dump the chilies in a bowl and stir in 2 cups of hot water. The chilies will need to be completely submerged in the water so you may need something to weigh them down.
2. Allow the chilies to soak 15 minutes until they become soft. Once soft, pure them in a blender until smooth.
3. Place the tomatillos, onions, tomatoes and garlic on the pan and roast them under your oven's boiler. Watch the vegetables carefully to ensure they don't burn and make sure to turn them regularly so that all sides are toasted in 15 minutes.
4. Mix the sugar, white vinegar, salt, puree from Step 2 and roasted vegetables together in a pot. Place the pot on the stove and bring the liquid to a boil while constantly stirring in 15 minutes.
5. Reduce the heat and let simmer until the liquid begins to thicken.
6. Transfer the salsa evenly between the jars, making sure to leave about 1/2-inch at the top of the jar. Secure the lids on each jar and process with the water bath canning Directions:for about 15 minutes.

Vegetable Beef Soup

Preparation Time: 5 Minutes | Cooking Time: 100 Minutes | Servings: 4

Ingredients:

- tbsp Italian seasoning mix
- 1 tsp black pepper
- 1 tbsp salt
- quarts tomatoes
- cups corn
- potatoes, cubed
- 1 cup celery, sliced
- 2 cups carrots, sliced
- 2 cups onion, chopped
- 2 quarts beef broth

Directions:

1. In a large stockpot, add 1 tsp olive oil and the meat. Cook until brown, then add the rest of the ingredients.
2. Simmer for 10 minutes, then ladle into jars. Process at 10 pounds pressure for 90 minutes.
3. Let cool for 12 hours before removal.

Chicken Soup

Preparation Time: 15 Minutes | Cooking Time: 95 Minutes | Servings: 3

Ingredients:

- 2 tsp black pepper
- 2 tsp salt

- tbsp garlic, minced
- 1 cup green onions, chopped
- cups carrots, sliced
- 1 cup celery, chopped
- cups raw chicken, chopped
- quarts chicken broth, or water with 4 chicken bouillon cubes

Directions:

1. Place broth or water and bouillon, as well as chicken, into a large stockpot. Bring to boil and add everything else. Bring to a boil and simmer for a few minutes.
2. Ladle into jars, leaving 1 inch headspace.
3. Process jars at 10 pounds pressure for 90 minutes. Let cool for 12-24 hours before removal and storage.

Bean and Ham Soup

Preparation Time: 25 Minutes | Cooking Time: 90 Minutes | Servings: 5

Ingredients:

- tbsp black pepper
- tbsp salt
- 14 cups water
- Large hambone (not neck bones)
- cups ham, chopped
- 1 cup onion, chopped
- 2 lbs 16 bean mix

Directions:

1. Soak beans overnight.

2. Add everything to a large stockpot, bring to boil.
3. Boil for an hour, then remove ham bone.
4. Ladle into jars, leaving 1 inch headspace. Process at 10 pounds pressure for 90 minutes.
5. Let cool for 12 hours before removal and storage.

Cabbage Beef Soup

Preparation Time: 25 Minutes | Cooking Time: 100 Minutes | Servings: 8

Ingredients:

- tsp dry celery
- 1 tbsp oregano
- tbsp basil, dried
- 1 tbsp parsley, dried
- tsp sea salt
- 10 turns fresh pepper
- 2 tbsp garlic powder
- 8 cups water
- 10 beef bouillon cubes
- 9 cups canned tomatoes with juice
- 2 cans light kidney beans
- 1 cup green bell pepper, chopped
- 1 cup celery, chopped
- 6 cups cabbage, shredded
- 2 cloves garlic, minced
- 1 large onion, diced
- 2 lbs ground beef

Directions:

1. Brown ground beef in a pan, scoop up 3 tbsp of grease for sauteing later.
2. Drain and wash beef to remove grease, optional.
3. Add water and beef bouillon cubes into a large bowl. Microwave for 5 minutes, stir briskly.
4. Pour 3 tbsp grease into a large stockpot and throw in onion and garlic. Sauté until tender.
5. Toss in all ingredients. Mix well, then bring to a boil, cover, and reduce to a simmer for 20 minutes.
6. Scoop up solid bits first, then ladle the liquid into each jar, leaving 1 inch headspace.
7. Process jars under 10 pounds pressure for 75 minutes. Let cool for 12 hours before removal and storage.

Pea Soups

Preparation Time: 35 Minutes | Cooking Time: 160 Minutes | Servings: 5

Ingredients:

- cup carrot, chopped
- 1 1/2 lbs ham shanks
- Salt and pepper
- 1 1/2 thyme, fresh, chopped
- bay leaves
- 1 bag dried split peas, rinsed
- cups water
- cups unsalted chicken broth
- 1 clove garlic
- 1 1/4 cups celery, chopped
- 1 1/2 cups yellow onion, chopped
- 1 tbsp olive oil

Directions:

1. In a large pot, heat olive oil. Add onion and celery, sauté for 3 minutes. Add garlic, sauté for another minute.
2. Pour in chicken broth and water. Throw in split peas, thyme, and bay leaves. Season with salt and pepper.
3. Add ham shanks, bring to boil, then reduce to low and simmer for 60 minutes.
4. Remove ham from soup, let rest for 10 minutes, then dice meat portion into pieces, cover.
5. Add carrots to soup, cover, and simmer for 30 minutes.
6. Stir ham back into soup, season as needed.

7. Ladle portions into jars, leaving 1 inch headspace. Process jars under 10 pounds pressure for 75 minutes.
8. Let cool naturally for 12 hours before removal and storage.

Apple Sauce

Preparation Time: 5 Minutes | Cooking Time: 30 Minutes | Servings: 2

Ingredients:

- Apples Water
- Granulated sugar, optional (For a tart flavor, add 1 to 2 lb (500 g to 1 kg) of tart apples to every 3 lb (1.4 kg) of sweeter apples)
- Organic product Fresh® Fruit Protector, optional

Directions:

1. Place the required number of clean 500 ml, 1 L or 1.5 L bricklayer cups on a rack in a boiling water canner; spread jugs with water and warmth to a stew (180°F/82°C). Put screw bands aside. Heat SNAP LID® fixing circles in high temp water, not boiling (180°F/82°C). Keep cups and fixing circles hot until prepared to utilize.
2. Wash, peel and center apples. To avoid browning, cut apples into a shading security arrangement made of 4 tbsp (60 ml) Fruit-Fresh® Fruit Protector disintegrated in 8 cups (2 L) water.
3. Drain apple cuts and place in a big stainless steel pan with simply enough water to anticipate staying. Mixing every so often to avoid staying, warm rapidly and cook approximately secured until apples are delicate – 5 to 20 minutes contingent upon assortment and development of apples.

4. For a smooth sauce, purée blend utilizing a food processor or food plant. For a stout sauce, coarsely crush half of the cooked apples; process remaining apples in a food processor or food factory. Return blend to a spotless pot.

5. Sauce might be stuffed with no additional sugar. In the event that craved, include 2 tbsp (30 ml) granulated sugar per 4 cups.

6. (1 L) fruit purée; taste and change in accordance with coveted level of sweetness. Spiced Applesauce – add ground flavors to taste, for example, cinnamon, nutmeg or allspice.

7. Stirring to avoid staying, convey fruit purée to a full moving boil (212°F/100°C) and keep up this temperature while filling jugs.

8. Ladle hot fruit purée into a hot cup to inside 1/2 inch (1 cm) of top of jug (headspace). Tenderly yet solidly tap cup on tea towel on counter to slacken air pockets AND then slide a nonmetallic utensil down within jug surfaces to discharge air boils. (This progression is imperative, as fruit purée normally traps a lot of air in the blend.) Wipe jug edge evacuating any food buildup. Focus hot fixing circle on clean cup edge. Screw band down until resistance is met, then increment to fingertip tight. Return filled jug to rack in canner. Rehash for residual fruit purée.

9. When canner is filled, guarantee that all jugs are secured by no less than one inch (2.5 cm) of water. Spread canner and convey water to full moving boil before beginning to check handling time. At heights up to 1000 ft. (305 m), heat handle the filled jugs for the time demonstrated underneath

Orchard Chili Sauce

Preparation Time: 5 Minutes | Cooking Time: 120 Minutes | Servings: 8

Ingredients:

- 5 cups (1250 ml) slashed tomatoes, around 2.5 lb (1.1 kg), 10 medium

- 3 cups (750 ml) slashed peaches, around 6 medium

- 3 cups (750 ml) slashed pears, around 3 large

- 1-1/2 cups (375 ml) slashed plums, around 10 medium

- 3 cups (750 ml) onion, slashed, around 1.5 lb (675 g), 3 large

- cup (250 ml) celery, slashed

- 1/2 cup (125 ml) red pepper, finely slashed

- 1/2 cup (125 ml) green pepper, finely slashed

- 2-1/2 cups (625 ml) solidly pressed brown sugar

- 1-1/4 cup (300 ml) juice vinegar

- Hot sauce, optional

- tsp (10 ml) pickling salt

- tbsp (30 ml) pickling zest
- 2 tsp (10 ml) celery seeds
- 12 inch (30 cm) cinnamon stick, broken
- 1/2 tsp (2 ml) entire cloves

Directions:

1. Wash, whiten, peel and cleave tomatoes; measure 5 cups (1250 ml). Wash, whiten, peel, center/pit and hack peaches and pears; measure 3 cups (750 ml) each. Wash, whiten, peel, pit and hack plum measure 1/2 cups (375 ml).
2. In a huge stainless steel sauce cup Mix tomatoes, peaches, pears, plums, onion, celery, red and green peppers, brown sugar, vinegar, hot sauce (to taste) and pickling salt.
3. Tie pickling flavor, celery seeds, cinnamon stick and cloves in a vast square of cheesecloth, making a zest sack; add to tomatoes. Heat blend to the point of boiling; mixing once in a while to avert searing, until blend achieves sought consistency, around 1and1/2 hours. Dispose of zest sack.
4. Place 8 clean 250 ml artisan cups on a rack in a boiling water canner; spread jugs with water and warmth to a stew (180°F/82°C). Put screw bands aside. Heat SNAP LID® fixing circles in high temp water, not boiling (180°F/82°C). Keep cups and fixing circles hot until prepared to utilize.
5. Ladle sauce into a hot jug to inside 1/2 inch (1 cm) of top of cup (headspace). Utilizing nonmetallic utensil, expel air boils and conform headspace, if required, by including more sauce. Wipe cup edge expelling any food buildup. Focus hot fixing circle on clean cup edge. Screw band down until resistance is met, then increment to fingertip tight. Return filled jug to rack in canner. Rehash for outstanding sauce.
6. When canner is filled, guarantee that all cups are secured by no less than one inch (2.5 cm) of water. Spread canner and convey water to full moving boil before beginning to tally handling time. At heights up to 1000 ft (305 m), process —boil filled jugs – 20 minutes.*
7. When handling time is finished, evacuate canner top, hold up 5 minutes, then expel cups without tilting and place them upright on an ensured work surface. Cool upright, undisturbed 24 hours; DO NOT RETIGHTEN screw bands.
8. After cooling check jug seals. Fixed circles bend descending and don't move when squeezed. Evacuate screw bands; wipe and dry bands and jugs. Store screw bands independently or supplant freely on jugs, as sought. Mark and store cups in a cool, dull spot. For best quality, use home canned foods inside one year.

Peach Rum Sauce

Preparation Time: 15 Minutes | Cooking Time: 40 Minutes | Servings: 6

Ingredients:

- 6 cups (1500 ml) arranged peaches, around 10 medium or 2 3/4 lb (1.25 kg)
- 2 cups (500 ml) daintily stuffed brown sugar
- 2 cups (500 ml) granulated sugar
- 3/4 cup (175 ml) rum
- tsp (5 ml) ground lemon get-up-and-go

Direction:

1. Place 7 clean 250 or bricklayer cups on a rack in a boiling water canner; spread jugs with water and warmth to a stew (180°F/82°C). Put screw bands aside. Heat SNAP LID® fixing circles in high temp water, not boiling (180°F/82°C). Keep jugs and fixing circles hot until prepared to utilize.
2. Blanch, peel, pit and slash peaches. Measure 6 cups (1500 ml).
3. Combine peaches, brown and granulated sugars, rum and lemon pizzazz in an big stainless steel pan. Heat to the point of boiling, blending until sugar breaks up. Boil tenderly, blending sometimes, until thick, around 20 minutes.
4. Ladle sauce into a hot cup to inside 1/4 inch (0.5 cm) of top of jug (headspace). Utilizing nonmetallic utensil, expel air boils and conform headspace, if required, by including more sauce. Wipe jug edge expelling any food deposit. Focus hot fixing plate on clean jug edge. Screw band down until resistance is met, then increment to fingertip tight. Return filled jug to rack in canner. Rehash for residual sauce.

5. When canner is filled, guarantee that all cups are secured by no less than one inch (2.5 cm) of water. Spread canner and convey water to full moving boil before beginning to number handling time. At elevations up to 1000 ft (305 m), process —boil filled jugs – 10 minutes.

6. When preparing time is finished, evacuate canner cover, hold up 5 minutes, then expel jugs without tilting and place them upright on a secured work surface. Cool upright, undisturbed 24 hours; DO NOT RETIGHTEN screw bands.

7. After cooling check cup seals. Fixed plates bend descending and don't move when squeezed. Expel screw bands; wipe and dry bands and cups. Store screw bands independently or supplant freely on jugs, as fancied. Name and store cups in a cool, dim spot. For best quality, use home canned foods inside one year.

Cranberry Sauce

Preparation Time: 15 Minutes | Cooking Time: 40 Minutes | Servings: 7

Ingredients:

- 4 cups granulated sugar
- 4 cups water
- 8 cups new cranberries (around 2 lb)
- Ground get-up-and-go of 1 big orange, optional
- 4 Ball®(16 oz) half quart or 8 Ball® (8 oz) half 16 ounces glass safeguarding cups with covers and bands

Directions

1. Get ready boiling water canner. Heat cups in stewing water until prepared for use. Try not to boil. Wash covers in warm lathery water and put bands aside.

2. Mix sugar and water in an large stainless steel pan. Heat to the point of boiling over high warmth, blending to disintegrate sugar. Boil hard for 5 minutes. Add cranberries and return blend to a boil. Decrease warmth and boil delicately, blending every so often, until all berries burst and fluid starts to sheet from a metal spoon, around 15 minutes. Blend in orange get-up-and-go, if utilizing, amid the most recent couple of minutes of cooking.

3. Scoop hot cranberry sauce into hot cups leaving 1/4 inch headspace. Expel air boils and change headspace, if fundamental, by including hot cranberry sauce. Wipe edge. Focus cover on cup. Apply band until fit is fingertip tight. Place cup in boiling water canner. Rehash until all cups are filled.

4. PROCESS jugs in a boiling water canner for 15 minutes, altering for elevation. Evacuate jugs and cool. Check covers for seal following 24 hours. Cover ought not flex all over when focus is squeezed.

Chapter 8: James & Jellies

Sweet Persimmon Jam

Preparation Time: 15 Minutes | Cooking Time: 40 Minutes | Servings: 40

Ingredients:

- 5 Cups of Persimmons, Pureed Variety
- 3 Cups of Sugar, White
- 1/4 Cup of Lemon Juice, Fresh
- 1/2 teaspoons of Orange Zest, Freshly Grated
- Dash of Nutmeg, Ground Variety

Directions::

1. Use a large sized saucepan and place over medium to high heat.
2. Add in all of your ingredients into your saucepan and bring to a boil.
3. Boil for the next 30 minutes or until your mixture is thick in consistency.
4. Remove from heat and allow to cool completely.

5. Pour your mixture into your canning jars and seal with your lids.
6. Boil your jars in some boiling water for the next 10 minutes. Remove and allow to cool slightly before placing into your fridge. Use whenever you are ready.

Sweet Crabapple Jelly

Preparation Time: 5 Minutes | Cooking Time: 15 Minutes | Servings: 31

Ingredients:

- 8 Cups of Crabapples, Fresh
- Some Water, As Needed
- 3 Cups of Sugar, White
- 1, 3 Inch Stick of Cinnamon, Optional

Directions:

The first thing that you will want to do is remove the stems and blossoms from your crabapples and then cut them into quarters. Place into a large sized saucepan.

1. Add in some water to cover and bring to a boil over medium heat. Allow to boil for the next 10 to 15 minutes or until they are tender to the touch.
2. After this time strain your apples and juice them. Discard any pulp and place your juice back into your pan.
3. Heat over low heat and allow to cook for the next 10 minutes. After this time skim off any foam that may appear on the top of your mixture.
4. Add in your sugar and stir thoroughly until completely dissolved.
5. Boil for the next 20 minutes before removing from heat. Allow to cool completely.
6. Pour your mixture into your canning jars and seal with your lids.
7. Boil your jars in some boiling water for the next 10 minutes. Remove and allow to cool slightly

before placing into your fridge. Use whenever you are ready.

Roasted Red Pepper Jam

Preparation Time: 15 Minutes | Cooking Time: 1 1/2 Hours | Servings: 35

Ingredients:

- 6 Pounds of Bell Peppers, Red in Color
- Pound of Tomatoes, Plum and Italian Variety
- Cloves of Garlic, Unpeeled
- 1 White Onion, Small in Size and Sliced Thinly
- 1/2 Cup of Vinegar, Red Wine Variety
- Tablespoons of Basil, Fresh and Finely Chopped
- 1 tablespoon of Sugar, White
- 1 teaspoon of Salt, For Taste
- Canning Jars, With Lids and Rings

Directions::

1. The first thing that you will want to do is roast your first 4 ingredients in your oven at 425 degrees until your ingredients are soft and black in color on all sides. Once black, remove from oven.

2. Allow your ingredients to cool completely before placing into a food processor and blending on the highest setting until smooth in consistency.

3. Place your mixture into a large sized saucepan and add in your remaining ingredients. Stir until completely combined. Heat over medium heat and bring this mixture to a boil.

4. Once your mixture is boiling, reduce the heat to low and allow to simmer for the next 20 minutes. Remove from heat and allow to cool completely.

5. Pour your mixture into your canning jars and seal with your lids.

6. Boil your jars in some boiling water for the next 10 minutes. Remove and allow to cool slightly before placing into your fridge. Use whenever you are ready.

Spicy Style Tomato Jam

Preparation Time: 5 Minutes | Cooking Time: 1 Hour and 40 Minutes | Servings: 4

Ingredients:

- 3 Pounds of Tomatoes, Fresh
- Gallon of Water, Boiling
- 1 Cup of Vinegar, Cider Variety
- 1/2 Cup of Apple Juice, Fresh
- 1 1/2 Cups of Brown Sugar, Light and Packed
- 1 1/2 teaspoons of Salt, For Taste
- 1/2 teaspoons of Black Pepper, Ground Variety
- 1/2 teaspoons of Mustard, Ground Variety
- 1/2 teaspoons of Allspice, Ground Variety
- 1/2 teaspoons of Cumin, Ground
- 1/4 teaspoons of Cayenne Pepper
- 1 Lemon, Cut into Quarters and Sliced Thinly

Directions::

1. The first thing that you will want to do is place your tomatoes into a large sized pot. Pour in your boiling water and allow to sit for the next 5 minutes. After this time remove your tomatoes and place into a cold water bath until completely cool.

2. Then chop up your tomatoes in a food processor, making sure to reserve any juices.

3. Next add in your remaining ingredients except for your lemon and tomatoes into a large sized saucepan and place over medium heat. Cook until your sugar fully dissolves.

4. Add in your chopped tomatoes and bring this mixture to a boil. Once boiling reduce the heat to low and allow to simmer for the next 30 to 45 minutes or until the liquid has been reduced by at least half.

5. After this time add in your lemon slices and continue to cook for the next 15 minutes.

6. After this time remove from heat and set aside to cool completely.

7. Pour your mixture into your canning jars and seal with your lids.

8. Boil your jars in some boiling water for the next 10 minutes. Remove and allow to cool slightly before placing into your fridge. Use whenever you are ready.

Sweet Tasting Kiwi Jam

Preparation Time: 15 Minutes | Cooking Time: 12 hours and 40 Minutes | Servings: 5

Ingredients:

- 24 Kiwis, Peeled and Thoroughly Mashed
- 3/4Cup of Pineapple Juice, Fresh
- 1/4 Cup of Lemon Juice, Fresh
- 3 Apples, Unpeeled and Cut into Halves
- 4 Cups of Sugar, White

Directions::

1. First use a large sized saucepan and bring together your first 4 ingredients. Set over medium heat and bring your mixture to a boil.

2. Once your mixture is boiling add in your sugar and stir thoroughly to dissolve.

3. Then reduce the heat to low and continue to simmer for the next 30 minutes.

4. Pour your mixture into your canning jars and seal with your lids.

5. Boil your jars in some boiling water for the next 10 minutes. Remove and allow to cool slightly before placing into your fridge. Use whenever you are ready

Onion Jam

Preparation Time: 15 Minutes | Cooking Time: 2 hoursServings: 2 pint jars

Ingredients:

- Onions – 1 lb
- Sugar – 1 cup
- White vinegar – 2 cups
- Water – 3/4cup
- Salt – 2 tbsp

Direction:

1. Chop the onions.
2. Combine sugar, water, vinegar on a low flame until the sugar dissolves.
3. Add the onions.
4. Bring to a boil and cook for 1 hour or until the onions are translucent.
5. Remove from heat and refrigerate once cool.

Pepper Garlic Jelly

Preparation Time: 5 Minutes | Cooking Time: 30 Minutes | Servings: 4

Ingredients:

- Peppers – 2 cups
- Jalapenos – 1/2 cup
- Garlic – 10 cloves
- Vinegar – 2 cups
- Sugar – 4 cups
- Pectin – 3 tsp

Direction:

1. Combine peppers, garlic and vinegar and bring to a boil.
2. Add sugar and pectin and boil until sugar dissolves.
3. Fill jars with the mixture.
4. Process in boilingwater bath for 15 minutes.

Fresh Tasting Papaya Jam

Preparation Time: 5 Minutes | Cooking Time: 5 Hours and 5 Minutes | Servings: 64

Ingredients:

- 5 Cups of Papaya, Ripe and Mashed
- 1/4 Cup of Orange Juice, Fresh
- 1/3 of a 1.75 Ounce Package of Pectin, Dry
- 5 Cups of Sugar, White

Directions::

1. First stir together your first 3 ingredients in a large sized pot placed over medium to high heat.
2. Once your mixture begins to boil, add in your sugar and stir constantly as it cooks.
3. Boil for at least 2 to 3 minutes before removing from heat and allowing to cool completely.
4. Pour your mixture into your canning jars and seal with your lids.

5. Boil your jars in some boiling water for the next 10 minutes. Remove and allow to cool slightly before placing into your fridge. Use whenever you are ready.

Simple Gooseberry Jam

Preparation Time: 15 Minutes | Cooking Time: 30 Minutes | Servings: 75

Ingredients:

- 2 Quarts of Gooseberries, Fresh
- 6 Cups of Sugar, White
- 1/2 of a 6 Ounce Container of Pectin, Liquid Variety

Directions::

1. First remove the blossom and stems from your gooseberries. Then puree your gooseberries until smooth in consistency.
2. Place into a large sized pot and add in your sugar.
3. Bring this mixture to a boil over high heat and allow to boil for at least one minute, making sure to stir constantly as it boils.
4. After this time remove from heat and add in your pectin. Stir to combine. Make sure to skim off any foam from your mixture. Allow to cool completely.
5. Pour your mixture into your canning jars and seal with your lids.
6. Boil your jars in some boiling water for the next 10 minutes. Remove and allow to cool slightly before placing into your fridge. Use whenever you are ready.

Lime *Jelly*

Preparation Time: 15 Minutes | Cooking Time: 40 minutes | Servings: 4

Ingredients:

- Limes – 10
- Water – 2 cups
- Sugar – 4 cups
- Pectin – 3 oz

Direction:

1. Grate the peel of the limes and squeeze the juice out of them.
2. Combine lime juice, peel, water, and sugar in a pan.
3. Bring to a rolling boil, stirring constantly.
4. And pectin and boil for 2 more minutes.
5. Ladle into jars and process in boilingwater canner for 10 minutes.

Strawberry Jam

Preparation Time: 5 Minutes | Cooking Time: 45 minutes | Servings: 4

Ingredients:

- Hulled and mashed strawberries – 3 lbs
- Lemon juice – 1/4 cup
- Powdered pectin – 6 tbsp
- Granulated sugar – 7 cups
- Butter – 1 tbsp

Direction:

1. Combine strawberries, butter and lemon juice in a saucepan.
2. Add pectin and bring it to a rolling boil. Do not stop stirring!
3. Add sugar and let it dissolve into the mixture. Boil for 1 minute.
4. Remove from heat.
5. Transfer hot jam into hot jars and process in boilingwater canner for 10 minutes.
6. Allow it to sit undisturbed for 36 hours.

Blueberry Jam

Preparation Time: 15 Minutes | Cooking Time: 2 hours | Servings: 3

Ingredients:

- Blueberries – 3 cups
- Sugar – 1/4 cup
- Lemon juice – 2 tsp

Direction:

1. Combine all the ingredients with a pinch of salt in a saucepan.
2. Mash until the juice oozes out of the fruit.
3. Cook for 20 minutes, until it thickens.
4. Refrigerate once cool.

Fig Jam

WATER BATH CANNING & PRESERVING COOKBOOK

Preparation Time: 5 Minutes | Cooking Time: 90 minutes | Servings: 4

Ingredients:

- Figs – 2 lbs
- Sugar – 1 1/2 cups
- Lemon juice – 1/4 cup

Direction:

1. Combine all ingredients and simmer for 6075 minutes, stirring continuously until it thickens.
2. Fill jars with the mixture.
3. Process in boilingwater canner for 10 minutes.

Pina Colada Jelly

Preparation Time: 15 Minutes | Cooking Time: 25 minutes | Servings: 2

Ingredients:

- Pineapple, chopped – 1
- Coconut cream – 1/3 cup
- Pectin – 3 oz
- Butter – 1/4 tsp
- Sugar – 3 cups
- Coconut – 1/2 cup

Direction:

1. Crush the pineapple and add it to a pot with pectin.

2. Pour coconut cream, sugar, and butter over it.
3. Boil for 10 minutes.
4. Pour into sterilized jars and process in boilingwater canner for 5 minutes.
5. Optional: you can use coconut rum or coconut water instead of coconut cream. Do not use coconut milk.

Lime and Blueberry Jam

Preparation Time: 5 Minutes | Cooking Time: 15 Minutes | Servings: 4

Ingredients:

- package of dry pectin
- 5 cups of sugar
- 1 tablespoon of lime zest
- 1/3 cup of lime juice

Directions

1. Crush blueberries one layer at a time, mixing with the pectin in a large saucepot.
2. Bring to a boil, stirring occasionally, and then add the sugar until it is dissolved.
3. Mix the grated lime peel and the lime juice, and return to a rolling boil.
4. Remove from heat, and put into jars.
5. Let the jars sit in a water bath for about 15 minutes.
6. Let cool completely before storing.

Raspberry Jam

Preparation Time: 15 Minutes | Cooking Time: 15 minutes | Servings: 5

Ingredients:

- 4 cups of raspberries
- package of pectin
- tablespoons of lemon juice
- 1/2 cups of sugar

JAMES & JELLIES

74

Directions

1. Crush the raspberries in a large saucepan, and put on high heat. Add the lemon juice and the pectin. Bring to a boil while stirring constantly.
2. Add the sugar and mix until dissolved. Let it cook for one more minute, and then remove from heat.
3. Pour the jams into the jars equally, cover, and let the jars sit in a water bath for about 10 minutes.
4. Let cool completely before storing.

Holy Habañero Hot Jelly

Preparation Time: 5 Minutes | Cooking Time: 15 Minutes | Servings: 4

Ingredients:

- 1/4 of a pound of bell peppers, about 12 peppers, any color
- 2 cups of cider vinegar
- 6 cups of white sugar
- 2 packets of pectin

Directions

1. Puree the peppers with vinegar in a food processor. Pour mixture into large saucepan, and add the sugar.
2. Let boil for about 10 minutes, stirring the whole time.
3. Put the hot jelly into the jars, and let them sit in a water bath for about 10 minutes.
4. Let cool completely before storing.

Cheery Cherry Jelly

Preparation time: 15 minutes | Cooking time: 1 hours | Servings: 4

Ingredients:

- 3 1/2 cups of cherry juice from about a bag and a half of cherries
- cup of water
- 1 package of pectin
- 4 1/2 cups of sugar

Directions

1. Crush freshly cleaned cherries in a large pot with the pits but no stems.
2. Add 1 cup of water, and boil over high heat.
3. Let it simmer for 10 minutes, and then strain it.
4. Throw out the pulp peels and pits, and then add pectin and stir.
5. Bring to a boil, add the sugar, and mix until dissolved.
6. Remove from heat, and put into jar
7. Let the jars sit in a water bath for 10 minutes.
8. Let cool completely before storing.

Blackberry Jam

Preparation time: 5 minutes | Cooking time: 10 minutes | Servings: 4

Ingredients:

- 4 cups crushed blackberries
- 4 cups sugar

Directions:

1. Place the crushed blackberries into a large stockpot. Add the sugar and let rest for 1 hour. Bring to a boil over mediumhigh heat, stirring constantly, until the mixture thickens. Remove the pot from heat and skim.
2. Pour the mixture into sterile jars and adjust the lids. Process for 5 minutes in boiling water bath.

Plum Orange Jam

Preparation time: 15 minutes | Cooking time: 5 minutes | Servings: 6

Ingredients:

- 10 cups chopped plums, skinless
- cup of orange juice
- 1 package pectin
- sugar cups
- tbsp. grated orange zest
- 11/2 tsp. ground cinnamon

Directions:

1. In a Dutch oven, combine orange juice and plums and bring to boil.
2. Reduce heat and simmer, covered, 57 minutes or until softened, stirring occasionally.
3. Stir in pectin. Bring to a rolling boil, stirring constantly.
4. Stir in cinnamon, sugar, and orange zest. Let boil for 1 minute, stirring until sugar completely dissolves.
5. Remove from heat and skim off foam.
6. Scoop the hot mixture in hot sterilized halfpint jars, leaving 1/4inch space of the top. Remove air bubbles and if necessary, adjust headspace by adding hot mixture. Wipe the rims carefully. Place tops on jars and screw on bands until fingertip tight.
7. Place jars into canner with boiling water, ensuring that they are completely covered with water. Let boil for 5 minutes. Remove jars and cool.

Figs and walnuts Jam

Preparation Time: 30 Minutes | Cooking Time: 15 Minutes | Servings: 8

Ingredients:

- 1/2 cups of water
- cup of granulated sugar
- 4 tablespoons of lemon juice fresh squeezed
- 5 cups figs chopped
- cups of chopped walnuts
- 1/8 teaspoon of cardamom

Directions:

1. Placing the figs into a heavy bottom pot. Add water to the jars and the pot until it reaches over the top of the jars. Bring the water to a boil over high heat. Turn off the heat and leave the jars in the water until ready to use.
2. Bring the sugar, water, and lemon juice to a boil in a medium pan over high heat. Reduce the heat to medium and cook for 5 minutes.
3. Add the figs, walnuts, and cardamom, reduce heat to medium-low and simmer for 10 minutes to lightly thicken.
4. Remove one jar from the canner at a time pouring hot water back into the canner. Place the jar on a soft towel or cutting board. Ladle the jam into the hot jar, leaving 1/4-inch headspace between the top of the jar and the jam. Using a damp paper towel, wipe the jar rim to remove any jam or residue around the lid. Repeat until all jars are filled.
5. Place the flat, round portion of the two-piece closure - in a small saucepan, cover with water and bring to a simmer over medium heat to sterilize the lids. Do not boil. Keep lids hot until you are ready to use them.
6. Carefully remove a lid from the hot water and place it on the jar. Place screw band on the jar. With your fingers, screw band down until resistance is met, then increase to fingertip-tight. Do not screw on tight.
7. Return the jar to the hot water-filled pot. Repeat lidding steps until all jars are in the canner. Adjust the water level in the pot so water is 1-inch above jars and bring water to a full rolling boil over high heat. Once the water

is boiling hard and continuously, begin the timing process of 10 minutes.

8. Turn off the heat and let the jars rest in the water for 5 minutes before removing. Remove the jars, lifting them out of the hot water and transferring to the towel or cutting board to cool. Once cooled, tighten the screw band, label and store in a cool dark place for up to 2 years.

9. Serve jam with toast or crackers, topped over pork, icecream and more.

Grape Jelly

Preparation Time: 15 Minutes | Cooking Time: 5 Minutes | Servings: 4

Ingredients:

- 4 cups of prepared juice (about 3 kilos of full ripe Concord grapes)
- 7 cups (3 pounds) of sugar
- 1/2 bottle of fruit pectin

Directions:

1. First, prepare the fruit. Root and crush about 3 kg of fully ripe grapes. Add

2. 1/2 cup of water; boil, cover for 10 minutes. Put it in the jelly cloth or bag and squeeze the juice. Measure 4 glasses in a very large pot. (If using wild grapes or other peel, use 3 1/2 cups of juice and add 1/4 cup of filtered lemon juice.)

3. To the juice measured in a pot, add the exact amount of sugar specified in the recipe. Mix well.

4. Put on high heat and boil, stirring constantly. Stir at once. Then bring it to a full boil for 1 minute, stirring constantly. Remove from the heat, filter the foam with a metal spoon, and quickly pour it into the glasses.

5. Process for 10 minutes after pouring into the sterilized jars

Apricot Amaretto Jam

Preparation Time: 5 Minutes | Cooking Time: 10 Minutes | Servings: 4

Ingredients:

- 41/4 cups peeled, crushed apricots
- 1/4 cup lemon juice
- 61/4 cups sugar, divided
- package powdered fruit pectin
- 1/2 teaspoon unsalted butter
- 1/3 Cup amaretto

Directions:

1. In a Dutch oven, combine lemon juice and apricots.

2. In a small bowl, combine pectin and 1/4 cup sugar. Stir into apricot mixture and add butter. Bring to a full boil over mediumhigh heat, stirring constantly.

3. Stir in the remaining sugar and let boil 12 minutes, stirring constantly.

4. Remove from heat and stir in amaretto.

5. Let the jam sit for 5 minutes, stirring occasionally.

6. Divide the hot mixture between eight hot sterilized halfpint jars, leaving 1/4inch space of the top. Wipe the rims carefully. Place tops on jars and screw on bands until fingertip tight.

7. Place jars into canner with boiling water, ensuring that they are completely covered with water. Let boil for 10 minutes. Remove jars and cool.

Apricot Jam

Preparation Time: 15 Minutes | Cooking Time: 40 minutes | Servings: 2

Ingredients:

- Apricots, chopped – 4 cups

- Lemon juice – 5 tbsp
- Sugar – 3 cups
  Direction:
1. Combine all ingredients and bring to a boil.
2. Simmer for 20 minutes, until it thickens.
3. Fill jars with the mixture.
4. Process in boilingwater bath for 10 minutes.

Mint Apple Jelly

Preparation Time: 5 Minutes | Cooking Time: 10 Minutes | Servings: 4

Ingredients:

- quart of apple juice, 2 pounds of sugar, a bunch of mint

Directions

1. Make 1 quart of apple juice: wash sour apples, dry them, put them in a pot, add water, and cook over medium heat. When the apples become soft, strain the juice without mashing the apples.
2. Bring the remaining juice to a boil, add a bunch of mint, and cook for 20 minutes.
3. Remove the mint, add sugar, and cook until the mixture thickens.
4. Remove from the heat, pour into jars, and wrap with parchment paper. Store at room temperature.
5. You can use the apple remains to make candy

Blackcurrant Jelly

Preparation Time: 15 Minutes | Cooking Time: 2 hours | Servings: 5

Ingredients:

- 2 pounds of berries
- 4 pounds of sugar

Directions

1. Prep the berries, blanch them, and pass them through a meat grinder in batches, adding sugar to the puree.
2. Thoroughly mix berries with sugar and let them sit for 34 hours. Then pack them into jars and seal.
3. Store in a cool place.
4. The jelly will turn out much better if you mash the berries with a wooden pestle or a spoon instead of passing them through a meat grinder.

Pineapple Jam

Preparation Time: 5 Minutes | Cooking Time: 10 Minutes | Servings: 4

Ingredients:

- 31/2 cups pureed pineapple
- 1/3 cup white rum
- cup cream coconut
- 1/4 cup lemon juice
- 6 oz. liquid pectin
- 6 1/2 cups sugar

Directions

1. Sterilize the jars.
2. Mix all the ingredients except the pectin and sugar in a saucepan.
3. Mix in the sugar.
4. Boil as you stir constantly for around 3 minutes.
5. Turn off the flame, mix in the pectin, and skim off any visible foam.
6. Ladle the mix immediately into the sterilized jars, leaving a quarter inch of headspace.
7. Get rid of any air bubbles and clean the rims.
8. Cover the jars with the lid and apply the bands, making sure that it is tightened.

9. Submerge the jars within a prepared boiling water canner and leave to process for 5 minutes.
10. Remove, allow to cool, and then label the jars.

Canned Pears

Preparation Time: 15 Minutes | Cooking Time: 2 hours | Servings: 5

Ingredients:

- lb. halved pears
- unsweetened apple juice, as required
- 1 cinnamon stick

Directions:

1. Sterilize the jar.
2. Cook the pears in water in a single layer until heated. Rinse and drain.
3. Place a cinnamon stick in the jar and pack the pears in it.
4. Bring the apple juice to a boil and then pour into the jar, leaving a halfinch of headspace.
5. Get rid of any air bubbles and clean the rims.
6. Cover the jars with the lid and apply the bands, making sure that it is tightened.
7. Submerge the jars within a prepared boiling water canner and leave to process for 20 minutes.
8. Remove, allow to cool, and then label the jars.

HerbFlavored Blackberry Jam

Preparation Time: 5 Minutes | Cooking Time: 10 Minutes | Servings: 4

Ingredients:

- 31/2 lbs. blackberries
- 1/4 cup sugar
- 2 tbsps. thyme
- 2 cups honey
- 13/4oz. powdered fruit pectin

Directions:

1. Sterilize the jars.
2. Place 1 cup of blackberries in a pot at a time and crush them until you get 6 cups of crushed blackberries.
3. Mix in the sugar and pectin.
4. Bring the mixture to a boil and cook, stirring until the sugar dissolves.
5. Mix in the honey and bring to a boil again.
6. Boil for a minute, stirring continuously.
7. Turn off the flame and skim off any visible foam.
8. Mix in the thyme.
9. Ladle the mix immediately into the sterilized jars, leaving a quarter inch of headspace.
10. Get rid of any air bubbles and clean the rims.
11. Cover the jars with the lid and apply the bands, making sure that it is tightened.
12. Submerge the jars within a prepared boiling water canner and leave to process for 10 minutes.
13. Remove, allow to cool, and then label the jars.

Tangerine Jelly

Preparation Time: 5 Minutes | Cooking Time: 30 Minutes | Servings: 4

Ingredients:

- 6 cups chopped tangerine pulp
- cup chopped lemon pulp
- 8 tbsps. orange zest
- 13/4oz. dry pectin
- 5 cups white sugar
- 1 cup water

Directions:

1. Sterilize the jars.
2. Combine the lemon pulp, tangerine pulp, water, and orange zest in a pot.
3. Boil, then simmer for 10 minutes on reduced heat, covered and stirring occasionally.
4. Strain using a moistened jelly bag and measure 4 cups of the juice.
5. Mix together the juice and the pectin in a saucepan.
6. Bring to a boil again and mix in the sugar, stirring until the sugar dissolves.
7. Bring to a boil again and boil for a minute.
8. Turn off the flame and skim off any visible foam.
9. Ladle the mix immediately into the sterilized jars, leaving a quarterinch of headspace.
10. Get rid of any air bubbles and clean the rims.
11. Cover the jars with the lid and apply the bands, making sure that it is tightened.
12. Submerge the jars within a prepared boiling water canner and leave to process for 10 minutes.
13. Remove, allow to cool, and then label the jars.

Lemon Tomato Jam

Preparation Time: 15 Minutes | Cooking Time: 1 hours | Servings: 6

Ingredients:

- 6 lbs. halved tomatoes
- 5 cups sugar
- 1/4 tsp. ground cinnamon
- 1/8 tsp. ground cloves
- sliced lemon

Directions:

1. Put lids and rings, 1 tbsp. distilled white vinegar, and water to cover in a saucepan.
2. Boil for 5 minutes then remove from heat and set aside.
3. Process the tomatoes in the food processor in batches until coarsely chopped.
4. Transfer them to a large heavybottomed stockpot as you work.
5. To the stockpot, add the sugar, cinnamon, cloves, and lemon slices.
6. Boil for 25 minutes over mediumhigh heat, stirring frequently to avoid scorching. Reduce the heat to low and simmer, continuing to stir frequently, for 30 minutes or until the jam begins to thicken.
7. Arrange the hot jars on a cutting board and ladle the hot jam into the jars, leaving a 1/4inch headspace. Remove any air bubbles and add additional jam if necessary to maintain the 1/4inch headspace.
8. Rinse the rim of each jar with a warm washcloth dipped in distilled vinegar.
9. Place the sealed jars in the water bather, ensuring each jar is covered by at least 1 inch of water.
10. Add 2 tbsps. white vinegar to the water and adjust the heat to high.
11. Boil and process both pints and halfpints for 20 minutes, then allow cooling.

Pear Jelly with Honey

Preparation Time: 5 Minutes | Cooking Time: 15 Minutes | Servings: 4

Ingredients:

- 12 medium ripened pears
- 2 tbsps. lemon juice
- 3 cups water
- 3 tbsps. lowsugar pectin
- 3/4cup honey

Directions:

1. Core the pears and coarsely chop them, leaving the skins on.
2. Transfer the pears to a large stockpot and add 3 cups of water. Simmer the pears for 10 minutes, covered, stirring occasionally.
3. Use a large spoon to place the pears in a damp jelly bag or in a strainer lined with several layers of damp cheesecloth. Let the juice drip for at least 2 hours or overnight. Don't squeeze the pears to make them drip faster; it will cause your jelly to be cloudy.
4. Add water to the canner to cover the jars. Boil the water, reduce the heat to low, place the jars in the water, and simmer until ready to use.
5. Combine the pear juice and lemon juice in a large saucepan. Gradually stir in the pectin until completely dissolved.
6. Leave the mixture to a full rolling boil over high heat, stirring constantly.
7. Add the honey and return the mixture to a full rolling boil for 1 minute as you stir.
8. Ladle the hot jelly into the canning jars, leaving 1/4 inch of headspace.
9. Remove air bubbles, wipe the rims, center the lids, and screw on the bands and adjust until they are fingertip tight.
10. Transfer the jars in the canner and bring to a boil. Make sure there is at least 1 inch of water covering the jars.
11. Process for 10 minutes, adjusting for altitude the allow cooling.

Rosemary Jelly with Vinegar

Preparation Time: 15 Minutes | Cooking Time: 10 Minutes | Servings: 6

Ingredients:

- 21/2 cups apple juice
- 3/4cup white balsamic vinegar
- 4 tbsps. classic pectin
- rosemary sprig
- 1/2 cups sugar

Directions:

1. Combine first 4 ingredients in a 4quart Dutch oven.

2. Allow the mixture to reach a full rolling boil that cannot be stirred down, over high heat, stirring constantly.
3. Add sugar, stirring to dissolve. Return mixture to a full rolling boil. Boil hard 1 minute, stirring constantly. Remove from heat. Discard rosemary.
4. Add the jelly into the prepared jar, leaving some space.
5. Clean jar rim and tighten the lid. Apply band and adjust to fingertiptight. Place jar in boilingwater canner. Repeat until all jars are filled.
6. Process jars 10 minutes then allow to cool.

Apricot Pineapple Jam

Preparation Time: 5 Minutes | Cooking Time: 30 Minutes | Servings: 4

Ingredients:

- 12 oz. dried apricots
- cup water
- 20 oz. crushed pineapple
- 1/2 cup grapefruit juice
- cups sugar

Directions:

1. Boil water and apricots in a big saucepan. Lower heat; cover. Simmer until apricots are very tender, for about 15 minutes. Mash. Add sugar, grapefruit juice and pineapple; simmer for 1 hour until translucent and thick, frequently stirring while uncovered.
2. Use boiling water to rinse lids and five 1cup plastic containers, then thoroughly dry. Put jam in containers; cool for 1 hour to room temperature. While covered, allow standing

until set or overnight, but for no more than 24 hours.

3. You can now use the jam. Freeze for up to 1 year or refrigerate for up to 3 weeks. Before serving, thaw frozen jam in the fridge.

Almond Apricot Jam

Preparation Time: 15 Minutes | Cooking Time: 30 Minutes | Servings: 5

Ingredients:

- 21/2 cups unsweetened apple juice
- cup diced dried apricots
- 1/2 tsp. almond extract
- 1/4 tsp. ground cinnamon

Directions:

1. Boil apricots and apple juice in a saucepan. Lower the heat and simmer until apricots are tender, for 2025 minutes, while uncovered.
2. Take off the heat; mash to preferred consistency. Mix in cinnamon and almond extract, and put into a pint jar and cover.
3. Refrigerate for 3 weeks maximum.

Canned Berry syrup

Preparation Time: 5 Minutes | Cooking Time: 50 Minutes | Servings: 4

Ingredients:

- 41/2 cups apple juice

- 11/2 cups honey
- 11/2 cups sugar

Directions:

1. Place the berries in a pot and crash them using a potato masher.
2. Add all other ingredients and bring them to boil at medium heat. Stir the mixture to ensure it doesn't overflow from the pot.
3. Reduce heat so that the mixture keeps on boiling over the next 40 minutes.
4. Fill sterilized jars with the syrup leaving a 1/2 inch headspace.
5. Clean the jar rims and place the lids on.
6. Transfer the jars to the pressure canner with water so that the jars are covered by water at least 2 inches.
7. Cover the pressure canner with an ordinary lid that fits well and process the jars for 10 minutes.
8. Remove the lids and let the jars rest in the canner for 5 minutes before transferring them to a cooling rack.
9. Label the jars before storing in a cool dry place.

Carrot Pineapple Pear Jam

Preparation Time: 15 Minutes | Cooking Time: 30 minutes | Servings: 5

Ingredients:

- 20 oz crushed pineapple, undrained
- 11/2 cups shredded carrots
- 11/2 cups chopped pears
- 3 tbsps. lemon juice

- tsp. ground cinnamon
- 1/4 tsp. ground cloves
- 1/4 tsp. ground nutmeg
- 1 package powdered fruit pectin
- 61/2 cups sugar

Directions:

1. Over medium heat, combine first 7 ingredients in a saucepan and bring to a boil.
2. Reduce heat and simmer, covered, until pears are tender (about 1520 minutes), stirring occasionally.
3. Add pectin. Bring to a full boil, stirring constantly.
4. Stir in sugar. Boil and stir for 1 minute.
5. Remove from heat and get rid of foam.
6. Scoop the hot mixture into halfpint jars (hot sterilized), leaving 1/4 inch space at the top. Get rid of excess air bubbles; add hot mixture to adjust headspace. Wipe the rims. Close the lids and tighten.
7. Set boiling water in a canner and set in the jars until fully covered. Allow to boil for 10 minutes. Set the jars aside to cool.

Rosy Jelly Retreat

Preparation Time: 5 Minutes | Cooking Time: 25 Minutes | Servings: 4

Ingredients:

- 31/4 cups white sugar
- 3/4cup grape juice
- 2 cups cranberry juice
- pack dry Pectin

Directions:

1. To make the jelly, take a heavy cooking pot and mix in the pectin and both the grape and cranberry juices in it.
2. Keep the heat on a medium setting, and let the mixture heat for few minutes.
3. Mix in the sugar. Stir the mixture and let it dissolve completely.
4. After that, remove it from the heat and remove the foam using a spoon.
5. Take the presterilized jars and place the grape jelly mixture into the jars.
6. Keep 1/2" margin from the top.
7. Use a damp cloth to clean jar rims; then close them with the lid and band.
8. Afterward, place the jars in the canning pot filled with water.
9. Set the canning timer at 10 minutes. Adjust the canning time based on your altitude level.
10. After the canning time is over, take out the hot jars, wipe them, and take off the bands.
11. Store in a dry, cool area and enjoy the delicious grape jelly!

Blushing Peach Jam

Preparation Time: 5 Minutes | Cooking Time: 60 Minutes | Servings: 4

Ingredients:

- Few drops of almond extract
- 6 oz liquid fruit pectin
- 7 cups granulated white sugar
- 1/4 cup lemon juice
- cups red raspberries, crushed
- cups peaches, peeled, pitted, crushed

Directions:

1. Add 2 tbsp lemon juice to the peaches, and another 2 tbsp to the raspberries. Combine with sugar in a saucepan. Mix well and bring to boil, boil hard for a minute.
2. Remove from heat and add pectin, stir and skim, and add a few drops of almond extract.
3. Pour into the jar, leaving 1/4 inch headspace. Then, process jars in boiling water for 10 minutes.

Mixed Berry Jam

Preparation Time: 15 Minutes | Cooking Time: 40 Minutes | Servings: 6

Ingredients:

- 3 cups sugar
- 4 1/2 tbsp fruit pectin
- 4 cups crushed berries of your choice

Directions:

1. In a saucepan, combine berries and gradually stir in pectin.
2. Put on high heat to bring to a rolling boil, stirring constantly.
3. Add sugar, stir to dissolve, bring to a boil again and boil hard for a minute, stirring constantly. Skim as needed.
4. Ladle jam into jars, leaving 1/4 inch headspace. Process jars for 10 minutes, then remove your jars and let cool for 12 hours before consumption or storage.

Caramel Apple Jam

Preparation Time: 5 Minutes | Cooking Time: 60 Minutes | Servings: 4

Ingredients:

- 6 cups fresh, peeled, diced apples
- 1/2 cup water
- 1/2 tsp butter
- 1/2 tsp ground cinnamon
- 1/4 tsp ground nutmeg
- package powdered fruit pectin
- cups sugar
- cups brown sugar

Directions:

1. In a Dutch oven, combine the apples, butter, water, nutmeg, and cinnamon. Cook, stirring, over low heat until apples are tender.
2. Stir in pectin. Bring to a boil.
3. Stir in sugar and let boil, stirring, for 1 minute.
4. Remove from heat and get rid of foam.
5. Scoop the hot mixture into half-pint jars (hot sterilized), leaving 1/4-inch space of the top. Get rid of excess air bubbles, add hot mixture to adjust headspace. Wipe the rims. Close the lids and tighten.
6. Set boiling water in a canner and set in the jars until fully covered. Allow to boil for 10 minutes. Set the jars aside to cool.

Candy Apple Jelly

Preparation Time: 5 Minutes | Cooking Time: 60 Minutes | Servings: 4

Ingredients:

- 4 cups apple juice
- 1/2 cup Red Hots candy
- package powdered fruit pectin
- 4-1/2 cups sugar

Directions:

1. In a large saucepan, combine the candies, apple juice, and pectin. Bring to a rolling boil, stirring constantly.

2. Stir in sugar and let boil, stirring, for 1 minute.
3. Remove from heat and get rid of foam.
4. Scoop the hot mixture into half-pint jars (hot sterilized), leaving 1/4-inch space of the top. Get rid of excess air bubbles, add hot mixture to adjust headspace. Wipe the rims. Close the lids and tighten.
5. Set boiling water in a canner and set in the jars until fully covered. Allow to boil for 5 minutes. Set the jars aside to cool.

Cucumber Jelly

Preparation Time: 5 Minutes | Cooking Time: 60 Minutes | Servings: 4

Ingredients:

- 2-1/2 cups cucumber juice, strained
- 7 cups sugar
- cup vinegar
- Seeds scraped from one vanilla bean.
- pouches pectin

Directions:

1. Mix first four ingredients in a pot and bring to a boil, stirring occasionally. Let boil for 2 minutes, then remove from heat.
2. Stir in the pectin, then return to a boil. Boil and stir for 1-2 minutes.
3. Remove from heat and get rid of foam.
4. Scoop jelly into half-pint jars (hot sterilized), leaving 1/4 inch headspace. Get rid of excess air bubbles, add hot mixture to adjust

headspace. Wipe the rims. Close the lids and tighten.
5. Set boiling water in a canner and set in the jars until fully covered. Allow to boil for 10 minutes. Set the jars aside to cool.

Cranana Tasty Jam

Preparation Time: 15 Minutes | Cooking Time: 15 Minutes | Servings: 4

Ingredients:

- 3 cups cranberries
- 1/2 cups water
- 2 cups pounded bananas
- 7 cups white sugar
- 1/2 (6 liquid ounce) cup fluid pectin
- teaspoon lemon juice

Directions:

1. In an large pan over medium warmth join cranberries and water; stew for 10 minutes. Mix in crushed banana and sugar. Increment warmth to medium-high; boil 1 minute. Mix in pectin and lemon juice.
2. Sanitize the jugs and tops in boiling water for no less than 5 minutes. Pack the jam into the hot, disinfected cups, filling the jugs to inside 1/4 inch of the top. Run a blade or a slender spatula around the internal parts of the jugs after they have been filled to evacuate any air boils. Wipe the edges of the cups with a damp paper towel to expel any food buildup. Top with tops, and screw on rings.
3. Place a rack in the base of a vast stockpot and fill most of the way with water. Heat to the point of boiling over high warmth, then painstakingly bring down the cups into the pot utilizing a holder. Leave a 2 inch space between the cups. Pour in additionally boiling water if essential until the water level is no less than 1 inch over the highest points of the jugs. Convey the water to a full boil, cover the pot, and process for 10 minutes.

Canned Strawberry Jelly

Preparation Time: 5 Minutes | Cooking Time: 5 Minutes | Servings: 3

Ingredients:

- 4 cups strawberry juice
- 71/2 cups sugar
- 2 pouches liquid pectin

Directions:

1. Wash the strawberries thoroughly, removing any stem or caps. Crush them and extract the juice.
2. Add the strawberry juice and sugar into a kettle. Give a good stir and heat until the mixture cannot be stirred down.
3. Add pectin and continue heating until it boils. Boil hard for a minute, then skim off any foam.
4. Pour the strawberry jelly into the sterilized jars, leaving a 1/4 headspace. Wipe the rims with a damp cloth and close the lids.
5. Transfer the jars to the pressure canner along with water so that the jars are covered by water at least 2 inches.
6. Cover the pressure canner with an ordinary lid that fits well and process the jars for 5 minutes.

Dandelion Jelly

Preparation Time: 5 Minutes | Cooking Time: 5 Minutes | Servings: 2

Ingredients:

- 4 & 1/2 cups of sugar, granulated
- 2 tbsp. of lemon juice
- 3 cups of tea, dandelion
- box of pectin, powdered

Directions:

1. Add the lemon juice, dandelion tea, and box of powdered pectin in a large-sized saucepan. Bring to boil.
2. Add sugar. Return to boil. Boil for one to two more minutes.
3. Remove mixture from heat. Fill jars, leaving 1/2" open at the top. The process by altitude (see chart in the introduction) and store in the refrigerator.

Elderberry Jelly

Preparation Time: 10 Minutes | Cooking Time: 22 Minutes | Servings: 4

Ingredients:

- 4 lb. crushed elderberries
- packet pectin
- 1/4 cup lemon juice
- 1/4 tsp. butter
- 41/2 cups sugar

Directions:

1. Add the crushed elderberries into a pot.
2. Place the saucepan over medium heat on the stove. Bring the elderberries to a boil while continuing to crush them.
3. Simmer for 10 minutes before removing the pot from the stove.
4. Strain the mixture through a sieve held over a clean pot. You want the juice of the berries to go into the pot.

5. Add the pectin following the instructions on the packet. Stir in the lemon juice.
6. Boil and stir in the butter and sugar. Continue constantly stirring until the jelly reaches a rolling boil. Continue to boil for 2 minutes.
7. Pour the jelly into the jars, leaving about 1/4 an inch of space in each jar. Attach the lids.
8. Process the jars using the water bath canning Directions:for 5 to 10 minutes.

Grape Plum Jelly

Preparation Time: 5 Minutes | Cooking Time: 20 Minutes | Servings: 3

Ingredients:

- 6 cups plums
- 5 cups black grapes
- cup water
- 1/2 tsp butter
- 8 1/2 cups sugar
- 1 3/4 oz powdered pectin

Directions:

1. Wash plums and de-pit them. Wash the grapes too.
2. Crush both the plums and the grapes together and mix with one cup of water in a saucepan.
3. Boil while covered, then simmer for 10 minutes.
4. Sift the mixture through two layers of cheesecloth, so it is dripping through to leave a juice.

5. Take 6 1/2 cups of the remaining juice and place in a saucepan, then add to the mixture. Boil the mixture over high heat for a whole minute and add the butter while constantly stirring.
6. Add the sugar and return to a boil, stirring constantly.
7. Spoon off the foam and start the canning process.
8. Leave a 1/4 inch of room at the top.

Holy Habanero Hot Jelly

Preparation Time: 10 Minutes | Cooking Time: 20 Minutes | Servings: 2

Ingredients:

- 1/2 lb. habanero peppers
- 1/4 lb. bell peppers
- 2 cups cider vinegar
- 6 cups white sugar
- 2 packets pectin

Directions:

1. Puree the peppers with vinegar in a food processor. Add the sugar to the mixture in a big pot.
2. Let this boil for about 10 minutes, stirring the whole time.
3. Put the hot jelly into the jars and let them sit in a water bath for about 10 minutes.
4. Let these cool completely before storing.

Apricot Lavender Jam

Preparation Time: 5 Minutes | Cooking Time: 35 Minutes | Servings: 2

Ingredients:

- 3 cups of apricots halved, pitted, and chopped
- 2 sprigs dried lavender flowers approx. 1/2 tsp - try 3/4 tsp for bolder flavor
- 1/4 cup of water
- 2 tbsp fresh lemon juice
- 1/4 cups of granulated sugar

Directions:

1. Abridge the apricots, lavender, water and the citric juice Bring the apricots, lavender, water, and lemon juice to a simmer in a medium-sized pot over medium heat, stirring occasionally. Reduce heat to low and cook, stirring periodically, for about 5 minutes, or until the fruit begins to soft

2. Cook, stirring, until sugar dissolves. occasionally, until the jam has thickened and the fruit has broken down, around 15-20 minutes. Any foam that has formed on the surface should be skimmed off and discarded.

3. Pour the jam into two half-pint mason jars that have been sterilized. Clean the rims with a damp cloth before screwing on the lids until they're finger-tight.

4. Hot water bath canning the jars Filling my biggest saucepan halfway with water and bringing it to a boil, just enough to cover the tops of the canisters. a quick boil Place the jars in the boiling water (with tongs or a container lifter) and wait 10-15 minutes for the lids to "pop" inwards, indicating that they have vacuum-sealed. The lids may not pop until the canisters have been removed from the water bath and allowed to cool.

5. Remove the water bath container and set them aside to cool. Deaths that are not in the center or bounce back haven't been properly sealed. Place the containers in the fridge first and eat them first.

6. Keep the rest of the jars in a dark, dry area for up to a year. Chocolate Cherry Jam

Preparation Time: 5 Minutes

Cooking Time: 16 Minutes | Servings: 6

Ingredients:

- 6 cups of fresh or frozen pitted dark, sweet cherries, coarsely chopped
- 6 Tbsp. Ball® Classic Pectin
- 1/4 cup of bottled lemon juice
- 6 cups of sugar
- 2/3 cup of unsweetened cocoa

Directions:

1. In a stainless steel of four-quarters or emailed Netherlands oven, mix the first three ingredients. Take the mixture to a full boil, stirring frequently. Meanwhile, whisk together the sugar and cocoa until smooth; add to the boiling cherry liquid all At the same time. Return to a full boil of the mixture. 1 minute of vigorous boiling, stirring continually Remove the pan from the heat.

2. If necessary, skim the foam. Fill a hot jar halfway with hot jam, leaving a 14-inch headspace. Air bubbles should be removed. Wipe the jar's rim. On the jar, place the lid in the middle. Apply the band and tighten it until it is fingertip-tight. In a boiling-water canner, place the jar. Rep until all of the jars are full. Adjust for altitude and process jars for 10 minutes. Remove jars from heat, remove lids, and set aside for 5 minutes. Set the jars aside to cool.

Mint Jelly

Preparation Time: 15 Minutes | Cooking Time: 47 Minutes | Servings: 5

Ingredients:

- 2 cups of fresh mint, firmly packed

- 2 cups of water
- 3 tbsp freshly squeezed lemon juice
- 31/2 cups of sugar
- 3 ounces liquid pectin
- 2 drops green food coloring

Directions:

1. Mix the mixer in a mixer jar mint and the water until the mint is finely minced. Fill a pot and bring it to a boil halfway through. Remove from heat and set aside for 45 minutes to steep. Using a fine-mesh strainer, strain the mixture into a dish, reserving the liquid (1 3/4 to 2 cups of). Mint should be discarded. Return the water to the bowl and mix.

2. lemon juice and sugar. Take a boil and reduce to a frying glass for 1 minute. Return to a boil with the pectin and cook for 1 minute.

3. Remove from the heat and add the food coloring. Skim the surface of the water. Allow to cool completely in a big container. Allow to chill overnight. Refrigerate for up to 5 days after transferring to a serving dish.

Apple Cinnamon Jelly

Preparation Time: 5 Minutes | Cooking Time: 60 Minutes | Servings: 4

Ingredients:

- 4 cups of unsweetened apple juice
- Powdered fruit pectin 1 package (1-3/4 ounces)
- 6-1/2 cups of sugar
- 2 tsp ground cinnamon
- 1/4 tsp ground cloves
- 1/4 tsp fresh ground nutmeg

Directions:

1. Mix apple juice and pectin in a Dutch oven. Bring a complete rolling boil over high heat, stirring frequently. Mix the remaining ingredients in a mixing dish. Return to a high rolling boil after stirring in the apple mixture.

2. 3 minutes of boiling and stirring Remove from heat and skim off any excess foam. Fill seven hot sterilized half-pint jars with the heated mixture, allowing 1/4-inch headspace. Clean the rims. Screw on bands until fingertip tight; center lids on jars.

3. Place the jars in a canner filled with simmering water, making sure they are completely covered. Take a boil and reduce to a frying glass for 5 Ten minutes. Ten minutes. Remove and chill the jars. Remove them.

Apricot Habanero Jam

Preparation Time: 5 Minutes | Cooking Time: 60 Minutes | Servings: 4

Ingredients:

- 3-1/2 pounds fresh apricots
- 6 tbsp bottled lemon juice
- 2 to 4 habanero peppers, seeded
- package (1-3/4 ounces) powdered fruit pectin
- 7 cups of sugar

Directions:

1. Apricots, pitted and chopped, should be placed in a Dutch oven or stockpot. Add the lemon juice and mix well. In a blender, mix the habaneros and a little portion of the apricot mixture. Process till smooth, covered. Return the pan to the stove. Add the pectin and mix well. Bring a complete rolling boil over high heat, stirring frequently.

2. Return to a full rolling boil after adding the sugar. 1 minute of boiling and stirring Remove from heat and skim off any excess foam. Fill 11

hot sterilized jars with the heated mixture, allowing a 1/4-inch headspace. Remove air bubbles and, if necessary, correct headspace by adding heated mixture. Clean the rims. Screw on bands until fingertip tight; center lids on jars.

3. Place the jars in a canner filled with simmering water, making sure they are completely covered. Bring to a boil, then cook Ten minutes. Ten minutes. Remove and chill the jars. Remove them. Allow 2 weeks for the jam to firm up at room temperature for optimum results.

Over-the-Top Cherry Jam

Preparation Time: 5 Minutes | Cooking Time: 60 Minutes | Servings: 4

Ingredients:

- 2-1/2 pounds fresh tart cherries, pitted
- Powdered fruit pectin 1 package (1-3/4 ounces)
- 1/2 tsp butter
- 4-3/4 cups of sugar

Directions:

1. Cover and process cherries in batches in a food processor until finely chopped. In a Dutch oven, mix the pectin and butter. Bring a complete rolling boil over high heat, stirring frequently. Return to a full rolling boil after adding the sugar. 1 minute of boiling and

stirring Remove from heat and skim off any excess foam.

2. Fill 6 hot sterilized half-pint jars with hot mixture, leaving 1/4-inch headspace. Remove air bubbles and, if necessary, correct headspace by adding heated mixture. Clean the rims. Screw on bands until fingertip tight; center lids on jars. Place the jars in a canner filled with simmering water, making sure they are completely covered. Take a boil, then cook for 5 minutes.

3. Remove the jars and set them aside to cool.

Pineapple-Rhubarb Jam

Preparation Time: 5 Minutes | Cooking Time: 60 Minutes | Servings: 4

Ingredients:

- 5 cups of sliced fresh or frozen rhubarb (about 12 stalks)
- 5 cups of sugar
- can (20 ounces) unsweetened crushed pineapple, undrained
- 1/4 cup of water

Directions:

1. Mix the rhubarb, sugar, pineapple, and water in a Dutch oven. Bring the water To a boil. - To a boil. Low heat; cover and cook for 18-22 minutes, or until rhubarb is soft, stirring periodically. Cook, stirring constantly, until the gelatin has dissolved. Remove excess foam from heat and skim. Fill heated half-pint jars halfway with the mixture, allowing a 14-inch headspace.

2. Remove air bubbles and, if necessary, correct headspace by adding heated mixture. Clean the rims. Screw on bands until fingertip tight; center lids on jars. Place the jars in a canner filled with simmering water, making sure they're thoroughly covered. Take a boil, then lower to a simmer minutes. Remove and chill the jars. Remove them.

Roasted Beet Jam

Preparation Time: 5 Minutes | Cooking Time: 60 Minutes | Servings: 4

Ingredients:

- 2-1/2 pounds fresh beets (about 10 small)
- tbsp canola oil
- 1 medium lemon
- 1 cinnamon stick (3 inches)
- 8 whole cloves
- 1 cup of sugar
- 1 cup of packed brown sugar
- 1/3 cup of maple syrup
- tbsp finely chopped crystallized ginger
- 1/8 tsp salt

Directions:

1. Preheat the oven to 400 degrees Fahrenheit. Beets should be peeled and sliced into wedges. Drizzle with oil and stir to coat in a 15x10x1-inch baking pan. Row the veggies for 50-60 minutes soft. Allow to cool slightly. Meanwhile, fill two 1-cup of plastic containers with hot water and clean the lids.
2. Thoroughly dry the area. Stand on a cutting board with the lemon straight and cut a thin slice from the top and bottom. Remove the skin and external membrane lemon using a knife. Slice in half. Remove the seeds from half of the lemon and thinly slice it (save remaining half for another use).
3. Cinnamon and cloves should be placed on a double thickness of cheesecloth. To surround the spices, gather the corners of the fabric and bind them tightly with twine. In a food processor, pulse beets until finely chopped.
4. Fill a big saucepan halfway with water. Bring to a boil the sugars, maple syrup, ginger, salt, chopped lemon, and spice bag. Reduce cook and heat to low, uncovered, 1 to 1-1/4 hours or until sauce has thickened. Remove the saucepan from the heat. spice bag. Allow to cool slightly.
5. Fill containers to 12 inches above the tops. Wipe the top edges of the containers clean, then cover them with lids right away. Cool till a week or freeze until ready. a year. Before serving, thaw frozen jam in the refrigerator.

Ginger Pear Freezer Jam

Preparation Time: 5 Minutes | Cooking Time: 60 Minutes | Servings: 4

Ingredients:

- 5-1/2 cups of finely chopped peeled fresh pears (about 10 medium)
- package (1-3/4 ounces) pectin for lower-sugar recipes
- tbsp lemon juice
- 1-1/2 tsp grated lemon zest
- 1 tsp minced fresh gingerroot
- cups of sugar
- 1 tsp vanilla extract

Directions:

1. Boiling water should be used to rinse seven 1-cup of plastic containers and lids. Thoroughly dry the area. Mix the pears, pectin, lemon juice, lemon zest, and ginger in a Dutch oven. Bring a complete rolling boil over high heat, stirring frequently. Add the sugar and mix well. Boil for 1 minute while continually stirring. Pour in the vanilla extract. Remove excess foam from heat and skim.Fill all containers to within 12 inches of the tops as soon as possible.
2. Wipe the top edges of the containers clean, then cover them with lids right away. Allow yourself to sit for 24 hours at room

temperature. Jam is now available for usage. Extra containers can be refrigerated for up to 3 weeks or frozen for up to 12 months. Before serving, thaw frozen jam in the refrigerator

Blackberry Apple Jelly

Preparation Time: 5 Minutes | Cooking Time: 60 Minutes | Servings: 4

Ingredients:

- 3 pounds blackberries (about 2-1/2 quarts)
- 1-1/4 cups of water
- 7 to 8 medium apples
- Additional water
- Bottled apple juice, optional
- 1/4 cup of bottled lemon juice
- 8 cups of sugar
- 2 pouches (3 ounces every) liquid fruit pectin

Directions:

1. Bring brown fruit and water to a boil Dutch oven. Slow to low heat and cook for 5 minutes. Set a sieve on a basin, bordered withfour layers of cheesecloth. Place the berry mixture in the sieve and cover with cheesecloth.
2. Allow to strain for 30 minutes, retaining the juice and discarding the pulp. Take the stalks and finish of the apples and discard them (do not pare or core them); chop them into tiny pieces. Add just enough water to cover in the

Dutch oven. Bring the water to a boil. Reduce heat for 20 minutes to low and cook. or until the apples are soft.

3. Using a cheesecloth-lined strainer, drain the juice while discarding the pulp. Return the blackberry and apple juices to the pan after measuring them. Add water or bottled apple juice to make 4 cups of if necessary. After that, add the lemon juice and sugar. Over high heat, bring to a full rolling boil, stirring frequently.
4. Add the pectin and mix well. Boil for another minute, stirring frequently. Remove excess foam from heat and skim. Fill nine hot sterilized half-pint jars with the heated mixture, allowing 1/4-inch headspace. Clean the rims. Screw on bands until fingertip tight; center lids on jars.
5. Place jars in simmering water in a canner, making sure they are well covered. Cook for 5 minutes and bring to boil. Remove and chill the jars. Remove them.

Triple Berry Jam

Preparation Time: 10 Minutes | Cooking Time: 15 Minutes | Servings: 2

Ingredients:

- cup strawberries
- 1 cup raspberries
- cups blueberries
- cups sugar
- 1 tsp citric acid

Directions:

1. Mix berries and add sugar. Set aside for a few hours or overnight. Bring the fruit and sugar to the boil over medium heat, stirring frequently. Remove any foam that rises to the surface. Boil until the jam sets. Add citric acid, salt and stir.
2. Simmer for 2-3 minutes more, then ladle into hot jars. Flip upside down or process 10 minutes in boiling water.

Red Currant Jelly

Preparation Time: 10 Minutes | Cooking Time: 50 Minutes | Servings: 2

Ingredients:

- 2 lb fresh red currants
- 1/2 cup water
- 3 cups sugar
- tsp citric acid

Directions:

1. Place the currants into a large pot, and crush with a potato masher or berry crusher. Add in water, and bring to a boil. Simmer for 10 minutes.
2. Strain the fruit through a jelly or cheese cloth and measure out 4 cups of the juice. Pour the juice into a large saucepan, and stir in the sugar.
3. Bring to full rolling boil, then simmer for 20-30 minutes, removing any foam that may rise to the surface. When the jelly sets, ladle in hot jars, flip upside down or process in boiling water for 10 minutes.

White Cherry Jam

Preparation Time: 5 Minutes | Cooking Time: 18 Minutes | Servings: 1

Ingredients:

- 2 lb cherries
- 3 cups sugar
- 2 cups water
- tsp citric acid

Directions:

1. Wash and stone cherries. Combine water and sugar and bring to the boil. Boil for 5-6 minutes then remove from heat and add cherries. Bring to a rolling boil and cook until set. Add citric acid, stir and boil 1-2 minutes more.
2. Ladle in hot jars, flip upside down or process in boiling water for 10 minutes.

Cherry Jam

Preparation Time: 5 Minutes | Cooking Time: 16 Minutes | Servings: 2

Ingredients:

- 2 lb fresh cherries, pitted, halved
- 4 cups sugar
- 1/2 cup lemon juice

Directions:

1. Place the cherries in a large saucepan. Add sugar and set aside for an hour. Add the lemon juice and place over low heat. Cook, stirring occasionally, for 10 minutes or until sugar dissolves. Increase heat to high and bring to a rolling boil.
2. Cook for 5-6 minutes or until jam is set. Remove from heat and ladle hot jam into jars, seal and flip upside down.

Oven Baked Ripe Figs Jam

Preparation Time: 5 Minutes | Cooking Time: 100 Minutes | Servings: 4

Ingredients:

- 2 lb ripe figs
- 2 cups sugar
- 1/2 cups water
- tbsp lemon juice

Directions:

1. Arrange the figs in a Dutch oven, if they are very big, cut them in halves. Add sugar and water and stir well. Bake at 350 F for about one and a half hours. Do not stir. You can check the readiness by dropping a drop of the syrup in a cup of cold water – if it falls to the bottom without dissolving, the jam is ready. If the drop dissolves before falling, you can bake it a little longer. Take out of the oven, add lemon juice and ladle in the warm jars. Place the lids on top and flip the jars upside down. Allow the jam to cool completely before turning right-side up.
2. If you want to process the jams - place them into a large pot, cover the jars with water by at least 2 inches and bring to a boil. Boil for 10 minutes, remove the jars and sit to cool.

Oven Baked Plum Jam

Preparation Time: 5 Minutes | Cooking Time: 2 hours & 10 minutes | Servings: 3

Ingredients:

- 4 lb plums
- 3 cups sugar
- cup water
- 1 tsp citric acid
- a pinch of cinnamon
- a pinch of ground cloves

Directions:

1. Halve the plums and take out the stones. Arrange them in a Dutch oven and cover with sugar. Add in water and bake at 350 F for 2 hours. Add citric acid and spices, ladle in hot jars and flip upside down.
2. If you want to process the jams - place them into a large pot, covers the jars with water by at least 2 inches and bring to a boil. Boil for 10 minutes, remove the jars and sit to cool.

Quince Jam

Preparation Time: 10 Minutes | Cooking Time: 45 Minutes | Servings: 3

Ingredients:

- 4 lb quinces
- 5 cups sugar
- 2 cups water
- tsp lemon zest
- tbsp lemon juice

Directions:

1. Combine water and sugar in a deep, thick-bottomed saucepan and bring it to the boil. Simmer, stirring until the sugar has completely dissolved. Rinse the quinces, cut in half, and discard the cores. Grate the quinces, using a cheese grater or a blender to make it faster. Quince flesh tends to darken very quickly, so it is good to do this as fast as possible. Add the grated quinces to the sugar syrup and cook uncovered, stirring occasionally until the jam turns pink and thickens to desired consistency, about 40 minutes. Drop a small amount of the jam on a plate and wait a minute to see if it has thickened. If it has gelled enough, turn off the heat. If not, keep boiling and test every 2-3 minutes until ready. Two or three minutes

before you remove the jam from the heat, add lemon juice and lemon zest and stir well.

2. Ladle in hot, sterilized jars and flip upside down.

Quince Jelly

Preparation Time: 15 Minutes | Cooking Time: 35 Minutes | Servings: 5

Ingredients:

- 3 lbs quinces
- about 4 cups sugar (enough to add a cup of sugar for every cup of juice)
- 6 cups of water
- 1/2 tsp citric acid

Directions:

1. Wash and cut the quinces, but do not peel them and keep the cores too. Put the quinces in a deep, heavy-bottomed pot and cover with water. Bring to the boil and simmer for 30 minutes. Strain the quince juice and measure it. It should be about 4 cups. Pour it in the pot

again and bring to a boil. Add the sugar - a little less than a cup for every cup of juice. Stir until the sugar dissolves, then simmer, skimming any foam off the top in necessary.

2. Cook the quince jelly until when you drop a small amount of it on a plate after a minute it has thickened. Add the citric acid, simmer for 2-3 minutes more and remove from the stove. Ladle in hot jars, and flip upside down.

Quince and Apple Jam

Preparation Time: 10 Minutes | Cooking Time: 30 Minutes | Servings: 5

Ingredients:

- 2 medium quinces, peeled and diced
- 3 large apples, diced
- 3 cups sugar
- 2 cups water
- 1/2 cup lemon juice

Directions:

1. Place the quinces, lemon juice, sugar, and water in a saucepan and bring to the boil. Simmer for 10 minutes, then add in the apples.

2. Simmer for 10 more minutes, or until the jam is set. Ladle into the warm, sterilized jars and seal. Flip upside down or process in boiling water for 10 minutes.

Apple and Blackberry Jam

Preparation Time: 10 Minutes | Cooking Time: 13 Minutes | Servings: 3

Ingredients:

- 2 lb blackberries
- 2 big apples, cut in cubes
- 5 cups sugar
- 4 tbsp lemon juice

Directions:

1. Place the blackberries and the apples in a saucepan and cover with the lemon juice and

sugar. Set aside for an hour. Bring to the boil, then reduce the heat and simmer until set. Remove from heat, add citric acid and stir. Boil for 2-3 minutes more and ladle into hot jars. Flip upside down or process 10 minutes in boiling water.

Aromatic Pear Jam

Preparation Time: 5 Minutes | Cooking Time: 10 Minutes | Servings: 3

Ingredients:

- 6 medium pears, diced
- 4 cups sugar
- 1/2 cup lemon juice
- 1/2 tsp cloves

Directions:

1. Combine fruit, sugar, lemon juice and spice and bring to the boil, stirring constantly until sugar is dissolved. Boil until jam is set. Ladle into hot jars and flip upside down or process 10 minutes in boiling water.

Pear and Apple Jam

Preparation Time: 5 Minutes | Cooking Time: 10 Minutes | Servings: 4

Ingredients:

- 2 big apples, diced
- 4 medium pears, diced
- 4 cups sugar
- 1/2 cup lemon juice
- 1/2 tsp cloves

Directions:

1. Combine fruit, sugar and lemon juice and spice and bring to the boil, stirring constantly until sugar is dissolved. Boil until jam is thick. Ladle into hot jars and flip upside down or process 10 minutes in boiling water.

Peach Jam

Preparation Time: 5 Minutes | Cooking Time: 60 Minutes | Servings: 4

Ingredients:

- 4 lb peaches, peeled, pitted and sliced
- 6 cups sugar
- 2 tbsp lemon juice

Directions:

1. Slice the peaches and combine them with sugar in a large pot. Bring to a boil, stirring gently, then lower heat to medium and simmer for 30 minutes, stirring constantly. Test if the jam is set by putting a small drop on a cold plate – it is set if it wrinkles when given a small poke with your finger. Skim any foam, add lemon juice and stir. Simmer for 2-3 minutes more, then ladle into hot jars. Flip upside down or process 10 minutes in boiling water.

Apricot Vanilla Jam

Preparation Time: 5 Minutes | Cooking Time: 10 Minutes | Servings: 1

Ingredients:

- 2 lb apricots, coarsely chopped
- 3 cups sugar
- tsp vanilla extract
- tbsp lemon juice

Directions:

1. Wash, stone and chop the apricots. Put them in a wide saucepan. Crack 6-7 of the stones and put the kernels in the saucepan too. Add sugar and stir. Bring gently to the boil and cook, stirring frequently, until thickened. Add vanilla and the lemon juice, stir and boil for a minute more. Carefully ladle into hot jars. Seal, flip upside down or process for 10 minutes in boiling water.

Pumpkin Jam

Preparation Time: 10 Minutes | Cooking Time: 70 Minutes | Servings: 3

Ingredients:

- 2 lb pumpkin, cut in cubes
- cup dried apricots, chopped
- 1 cup raisins
- cups sugar
- 1 tsp citric acid

Directions:

1. Cut the pumpkin and put it in a wide saucepan. Cover with sugar, stir and leave overnight or for a few hours. Add apricots and raisins. Slowly bring to the boil, then simmer, stirring frequently, until the pumpkin is tender. Add citric acid, boil for a few minutes more and gently ladle in jars. Flip upside down or process for 10 minutes in boiling water.

Caramelized Onion Jam

Preparation Time: 10 Minutes | Cooking Time: 37 Minutes | Servings: 4

Ingredients:

- lb red onions, thinly sliced
- 1/2 cup water
- tbsp olive oil
- 1 spring fresh thyme
- tbsp brown sugar
- tbsp balsamic vinegar

Directions:

1. Heat olive oil in a saucepan over medium heat. Add onions and thyme. Cook, stirring occasionally, for 15-20 minutes or until golden. Add sugar and continue cooking for 3 minutes. Add in vinegar and 1/2 cup cold water. Bring to the boil, reduce heat to low and simmer, uncovered, for 5 minutes or until thick. Ladle in hot jars, flip upside down or process in boiling water for 10 minutes.

Chapter 9: Strawberry Freeze Jam

Strawberry Tasty Jam

Preparation Time: 5 Minutes | Cooking Time: 4 Minutes | Servings: 3

Ingredients:

- 2 cups pulverized new strawberries
- 4 cups sugar 1 (1.75 ounce) bundle dry pectin
- 3/4 cup water

Directions:

1. Blend pulverized strawberries with sugar, and let stand for 10 minutes. In the interim, blend the pectin into the water in a little pan. Heat to the point of boiling over medium-high warmth, and boil for 1 minute. Blend the boiling water into the strawberries. Permit to remain for 3 minutes before filling jugs or other stockpiling cups.
2. Place tops on the cups, and leave for 24 hours. Place into cooler, and store solidified until prepared to utilize.

Rhubarb Strawberry Jam

Preparation Time: 5 Minutes | Cooking Time: 12 Minutes | Servings: 2

Ingredients:

- 5 cups cleaved new rhubarb
- 3 cups white sugar
- (3 ounce) bundle strawberry

Directions:

1. In a heavypot or stockpot, blend together the crisp rhubarb and sugar. Cover, and let stand overnight.

2. Heat the rhubarb and sugar to the point of boiling over medium warmth. Boil, blending always, for 12 minutes on low warmth. Expel from warmth, and mix in dry gelatin blend. Exchange to sterile cups, and refrigerate.

Jalapeno Strawberry Jam

Preparation Time: 15 Minutes | Cooking Time: 17 Minutes | Servings: 6

Ingredients:

- 4 cups crushed strawberries
- cup minced jalapeno peppers
- 1/4 cup lemon juice
- 1 (2 ounce) bundle powdered natural product pectin
- 7 cups white sugar
- 8 half 16 ounces canning cups with covers and rings

Directions:

1. Place the pulverized strawberries, minced jalapeno pepper, lemon juice, and pectin into an big pot, and heat to the point of boiling over high warmth. When stewing, blend in the sugar until disintegrated, come back to a boil, and cook for 1 minute.

2. Disinfect the jugs and tops in boiling water for no less than 5 minutes. Pack the jam into the hot, disinfected cups, filling the jugs to inside 1/4 inch of the top. Run a blade or a slender spatula around the inner parts of the jugs after they have been filled to expel any air boils. Wipe the edges of the jugs with a soggy paper towel to evacuate any food deposit. Top with covers, and screw on rings.

3. Place a rack in the base of a vast stockpot and fill most of the way with water. Heat to the point of boiling over high warmth, then deliberately bring down the cups into the pot utilizing a holder. Leave a 2 inch space between the jugs. Pour in all the more boiling water if important until the water level is no less than 1 inch over the highest points of the cups. Convey the water to a full boil, cover the pot, and process for 10 minutes.

4. Expel the jugs from the stockpot and spot onto a fabric secured or wood surface, a few crawls separated. Permit to cool overnight Once cool, press the highest point of every cover with a finger, guaranteeing that the seal is tight (top does not climb or down by any stretch of the imagination). Store in a cool, dim territory.

Chapter 10: Fermented Recipes

Lacto-Fermented Carrot-Apple Blend

Preparation Time: 5 Minutes | Cooking Time: 0 | Servings: 4

Ingredients:

- 4 cups sliced carrots
- 4 medium-ripe apples, cored then chopped
- Slice bunch green onions thin
- 8 tablespoons sea salt Saltwater
- brine, depending on the need

Directions:

1. In a food processor, combine the carrots, green onions, and apples. Blend several times until you get a smooth mixture. Then, add the ginger and salt. Place the mixture in jars. Press the ingredients down until they are compacted. Leave 1 inch headspace.
2. Saltwaterbrine can be added to the mixture if the natural juices don't cover it. Use a plate or a weighted lid to weigh the ingredients and then cover with a towel. Allow the jar to rest at room temperature for three to five days before fermentation. Place the jar in the fridge and let it cool for up to two months

Coconut Yogurt

Preparation Time: 20 Minutes | Cooking Time: 12 hours | Servings: 4

Ingredients:

- 8 cups coconut milk
- Starter yogurt culture
- 3 tablespoons gelatin
- 2 tablespoons raw honey
- 2 teaspoons vanilla extract

Directions:

1. Pour the coconut milk into a saucepan and heat to 180°F then removefrom heat and cool to 105°F.
2. Transfer the milk to a large glass jar, reserving 1 cup of it. Whisk the starter culture into the reserved cup of milk.
3. Stir the milk mixture into the milk in the jar then place it in a yogurtmaker.
4. Let the yogurt brew for 8 to 12 hours then remove from the yogurtmaker. Bring 2 tablespoons of water to boil in a small saucepan.
5. Whisk in the gelatin, honey and vanilla extract then whisk the mixtureinto the yogurt.
6. Divide the yogurt among glass jars then chill for 6 to 8 hours until itforms a clean break. Blend the yogurt in a blender until smooth then store in the refrigerator.

Fermented Lemonade

Preparation Time: 5 Minutes | Cooking Time: 0

Servings: 4 |

Ingredients:

- 6 lemons, juiced
- 1/2 cup organic cane sugar
- 1/2 cup whey
- Filtered water, as needed

Directions:

1. Whisk together the lemon juice, sugar and whey in a large glass jar. 2. Stir in the filtered water until the sugar dissolves.

2. Add enough water to fill the jar within 1 inch of the top then cover
3. witha lid.
4. Cover the jar with a clean towel then let rest at room temperature for 2 days.
5. Transfer the jar to the refrigerator to store.

Kombucha

Preparation Time: 5 Minutes | Cooking Time: 4 Minutes | Servings: 8

Ingredients:

- 15 cups filtered water
- cup organic cane sugar
- tablespoons loose-leaf tea
- cups store-bought kombucha
- 1 scoby

Directions:

1. Bring the water to boil in a medium saucepan then remove from heat. 2. Stir in the loose-leaf tea and sugar until the sugar is dissolved then coolto room temperature.
2. Strain the mixture into a large glass pitcher then stir in 12 cups ofwater.
3. Add in the prepared kombucha and pour the mixture into a large glassjar.
4. Add the scoby then cover the jar with cloth and let rest at roomtemperature for 7 to 10 days until it reaches the desired flavor 6.
5. Pour the kombucha into glass bottles and chill before serving.:

Fermented Orange Juice

Preparation Time: 5 Minutes | Cooking Time: 0

Servings: 2 | Ingredients:

- 2 tablespoons whey
- Pinch sea
- Salt
- Filtered water, as needed

Directions:

1. Whisk together the orange juice, whey, and salt then pour into a glassjar.
2. Add about 1 cup of filtered water or enough to fill the jar within 1 inchof the top.
3. Cover the jar tightly and shake then store at room temperature for 48 hours.
4. Transfer the jar to the refrigerator and chill before serving.

Fermented Raspberry Lemonade

Preparation Time: 5 Minutes | Cooking Time: 10 Minutes | Servings: 4

Ingredients:

- 1/2 cups filtered water
- 1/2 cups fresh raspberries
- 1/2 cup raw honey
- 1 1/2 cups fresh lemon juice
- 4 cups prepared kombucha

Directions:

1. Combine the water, raspberries, and honey to a saucepan and simmerfor 10 minutes until tender.
2. Transfer the mixture to a blender and add the lemon juice.
3. Blend the mixture until smooth then pour the mixture into a large glasspitcher.
4. Add the kombucha and stir well then serve immediately.

Water Kefir

Preparation Time: 5 Minutes | Cooking Time: 5 Minutes | Servings: 5

Ingredients:

- 6 cups filtered water
- 1/4 cup organic cane sugar
- 1/4 cup water kefir grains
- 2 dried figs
- ripe lemon, quartered

Directions:

1. Bring the water to boil in a large saucepan then whisk in the sugar andstir until dissolved.
2. Remove from heat and cool the mixture to room temperature.
3. Pour the water kefir grains into a large jar then stir in the sugar water.
4. Add the lemon and figs then cover the jar with the lid.
5. Let the jar rest at room temperature for 2 to 3 days until fermented.
6. Strain the mixture into a pitcher, discarding the lemons and figs thenchill before enjoying.

Kefir Iced Tea

Preparation Time: 15 Minutes | Cooking Time: 5 Minutes | Servings: 5

Ingredients:

- 6 cups filtered water

- 1/4 cup organic cane sugar
- 1/4 cup water kefir grains
- ripe lemon, leaves
- Handful fresh mint leaves
- Boiling water, as needed

Directions:

1. Bring the water to boil in a large saucepan then whisk in the sugar andstir until dissolved.
2. Remove from heat and cool the mixture to room temperature.
3. Pour the water kefir grains into a large jar then stir in the sugar water.
4. Add the lemon then cover the jar with the lid.
5. Let the jar rest at room temperature for 2 to 3 days until fermented.
6. Place the mint in a bowl and pour the boiling water over it.
7. Let steep for at least 15 minutes then strain and cool to roomtemperature.
8. Mix 1 part mint tea with 1 part water kefir and serve chilled.

Healthy Wine Jelly

Preparation Time: 5 Minutes | Cooking Time: 5 Minutes | Servings: 3

Ingredients:

- 3 1/2 cups wine
- 1/2 cup crisp lemon juice
- (2 ounce) bundle dry pectin
- 4 1/2 cups white sugar

Directions:

1. Join wine, lemon juice, and pectin in an large saucepot. Heat to the point of boiling, mixing often. Include sugar, blending until broke down. Come back to a moving boil. Boil hard 1 minute, blending always. Expel from warmth. Skim froth off top, if vital.
2. Spoon hot jam into hot, sanitized jugs, leaving 1/2 inch headspace. Fix 2 piece covers. Process for 5 minutes in boiling water shower.

Grape Wine

Preparation Time: 15 Minutes | Cooking Time: 10 Minutes | Servings: 4

Ingredients:

- pounds black grapes, washed
- 4 tablespoons wheat kernels
- 1.1 pounds sugar
- 1/2 teaspoon instant yeast

3 cups water, boiled, cooled completely

Directions:

1. Dry the grapes by patting with a towel. Make sure the grapes are absolutely dry. Crush the grapes in a bowl, using your hand.
2. Transfer the grapes into the pot. Add wheat kernels, sugar, instant yeast and water and stir until sugar dissolves completely. Tighten the lid.
3. Store in a cool and dark place for 3 weeks. Remember to note the day of making the wine.
4. Stir the wine with a wooden ladle every day at almost the same, for the first 19 days. Do not stir on the 20th day.
5. On the 21st day strain the clear wine, making sure not to disturb the deposits at the bottom of the jar. Pour the strained wine into another jar. Fasten the lid and keep it in a cool and dark place for another 7 days. Do not disturb the jar during this time.
6. Pour into fancy, colored glass bottles, making sure not to disturb the deposits at the bottom of the jar. Put the corks on the bottles.

7. You can add about a tablespoon of rum to the strained wine before pouring into the bottles. This will prevent further fermentation.
8. Make sure to label the bottles with the date of preparing and name.
9. Place in the refrigerator, serve chilled.

White Wine

Preparation Time: 5 Minutes | Cooking Time: 20 Minutes | Servings: 5

Ingredients:

- pounds white wine grapes, washed 4 times
- 6 cups water, boiled, cooled
- 1/2 tablespoon yeast
- 1/2 teaspoon sugar, to activate yeast
- pounds sugar
- 1/4 cup lukewarm water

Directions:

1. Pour water into the glass jar. Add 2.75 pounds sugar and stir with a wooden spoon, until sugar dissolves completely.
2. Dry the grapes by patting with a towel. Make sure the grapes are absolutely dry.
3. Crust the grapes in a food processor or grinder and add into the jar of sugar solution.
4. Add 1/2 teaspoon sugar and 1/4 cup lukewarm water into a bowl and stir until sugar dissolves completely.
5. Stir in the yeast. Cover and set aside for 10 minutes. By the end of 10 minutes the mixture should be frothy. Add this mixture into the jar. Mix well. Tighten the lid.
6. Remember to note the day of making the wine. Place the jar in a warm area.
7. In 12 – 15 hours, bubbles should be visible. Stir well once again and keep the jar covered with cotton cloth. Place the lid on the jar, very partially opened.
8. Stir once every day for 6 – 7 days.
9. Strain the mixture and place in another jar. Tighten the lid and keep it in a cool and dark place for a month. Do not disturb the jar during this time.

10. Pour into fancy, colored glass bottles, making sure not to disturb the deposits at the bottom of the jar. Put the corks on the bottles.
11. Make sure to label the bottles with the date of preparing and name.
12. Set aside the bottles for 6 months in a cool and dark area to mature.

Christmas Wine

Preparation Time: 5 Minutes | Cooking Time: 60 Minutes | Servings: 4

Ingredients:

- pounds grapes, washed
- 8 tablespoons wheat kernels
- pounds sugar
- 3/4 teaspoon instant yeast
- 6 cups water, boiled, cooled completely
- 4 whole cloves
- 8 cardamom pods
- stick cinnamon
- 1 1/2 teaspoons rum
- 1/2 cup lukewarm water

Directions:

1. Dry the grapes by patting with a towel. Make sure the grapes are absolutely dry. Crush the grapes in a bowl, using your hand.
2. Transfer the grapes into the pot. Scatter half the sugar over the grapes. Scatter the whole spices and wheat kernels, rum, instant yeast and water.

3. Keep the jar covered with a cotton cloth and place it in a cool and dark area, for 21 days.
4. Stir once every day.
5. On the 21st day strain the clear wine, making sure not to disturb the deposits at the bottom of the jar. Pour the strained wine into another jar.
6. Taste the wine and add as much as required, the remaining sugar to suit your taste. Fasten the lid and keep it in a cool and dark place for another 15 - 20 days.
7. Pour the wine into another jar every 2 – 3 days (during these 15 – 20 days), without disturbing the sediments. Discard the sediments. Do this until your wine is clear.
8. Pour wine into fancy, colored glass bottles, making sure not to disturb the deposits at the bottom of the jar. Put the corks on the bottles.
9. Make sure to label the bottles with the date of preparation and name.
10. Chill until use.

Strawberry Wine

Preparation Time: 5 Minutes | Cooking Time:0 | Servings: 4

Ingredients:

- 2 – 2 1/2 pounds strawberries
- 1/2 teaspoon acid blend
- 1/4 teaspoon pectic enzyme
- 1/2 packet wine yeast
- pound sugar
- 1/8 teaspoon tannin
- Water, as required

Directions:

1. Stir together sugar and strawberries in the fermentation container. Set aside for 5 – 6 hours for the juices to release.
2. Stir in acid blend, pectic enzyme and tannin. Add about 6 – 8 cups of water. Stir well.
3. Combine yeast and about 2 tablespoons lukewarm water in a bowl. Set aside for 5 minutes.
4. Pour into the strawberry mixture. Stir well.
5. Close the jar with the fermentation lid. If you do not have fermentation lids, cover the jar

with cheesecloth. Remember to note the day of preparing.

6. Place the jar at room temperature for 14 days.

7. Strain the mixture into another fermentation container with a fine wire mesh strainer. Do not strain the sediments.

8. Close the jar with the fermentation lid. Set aside in a cool and dark place for 6 weeks.

9. Pour into fancy, colored glass bottles, making sure not to disturb the sediments at the bottom of the jar. Put the corks on the bottles.

10. Make sure to label the bottles with the date of preparation and name.

11. Set aside the bottles for 4 – 6 months in a cool and dark area to mature.

Blackberry Wine

Preparation Time: 5 Minutes | Cooking Time: 12 hours | Servings: 4

Ingredients:

- 2 1/4 pounds blackberries
- 1/2 package red wine yeast
- 1/2 tablespoon yeast nutrient
- 1/2 pounds granulated sugar
- 1/2 tablespoon pectic enzyme
- 4 1/2 cups boiling water

Directions:

1. Place blackberries in a sterilized brew bin and crush the berries using a potato masher or with your hands. Do not over-mash the berries.

2. Pour 2 cups boiling water into the brew bin and mix well. Once it cools, stir in pectic enzyme. Keep the bin covered and set aside on your countertop for 12 hours.

3. Combine sugar and remaining boiling water in a bowl. Stir until sugar dissolves completely. Pour the sugar solution into the brew bin and stir. Let the mixture cool completely.

4. Stir in yeast nutrient and red wine yeast. Close the lid and place the bin in a cool and dark area.

5. Stir the mixture every day. Do this for 4 to 5 days.

6. Place a strainer over another sterilized brew bin. Strain the mixture into the bin.

7. Pour the strained mixture into a Demi-John. Seal the bottle and place it in a cool and dark area.

8. After 6 weeks, pour into another Demi-john (do not add the sediments) and place it in a cool and dark area.

9. After 6 – 8 weeks, pour into another Demi-John and place it in a cool and dark area.

10. After 2 – 6 weeks, when you are satisfied with the fermentation, pour into fancy colored glass bottles. Put the corks on the bottles.

11. Make sure to label the bottles with the date of preparation and name.

12. Set aside the bottles for 4 – 6 months in a cool and dark area, to mature.

Raspberry Wine

Preparation Time: 20 Minutes | Cooking Time: 15 Minutes | Servings: 2

Ingredients:

- 1/2 - 2 pounds raspberries
- Juice of 1/2 lemon
- 1/2 tablespoon yeast nutrient
- 1 pound granulated sugar
- 1/2 packet wine yeast
- 8 cups water

Directions:

1. Add water and sugar into a saucepan and place the saucepan over medium flame. Boil the water and stir frequently until sugar dissolves. Turn off the heat and let it cool completely.

2. Pour into a sterilized brew bin container. Stir in the raspberries. Set aside for an hour.

3. Stir in lemon juice and yeast nutrient. Cover and set aside in a cool and dark place.

4. After 24 hours, stir in white wine yeast and set aside for 24 hours.

5. Place a strainer over another sterilized brew bin. Strain the mixture into the bin.

6. Pour the strained mixture into a Demi-John. Seal the bottle and place it in a cool and dark area.

7. After 6 to 7 days, when active fermentation has stopped, pour into another Demi-john (do not add the sediments) and place it in a cool and dark area.

8. After 6 – 8 weeks, pour into another Demi-John and place it in a cool and dark area. If you are satisfied with the taste, pour into fancy, colored glass bottles, making sure not to add sediments. Go to step 10.Else pour it into a Demi-John bottle set aside for 2 weeks.

9. After 2 weeks, when you are satisfied with the fermentation, pour into fancy colored glass bottles.

10. Put the corks on the bottles.

11. Make sure to label the bottles with the date of preparing and name.

12. Set aside the bottles for 4 – 6 months in a cool and dark area, to mature.

Blueberry Wine

Preparation Time: 5 Minutes | Cooking Time: 10 Minutes | Servings: 7
Ingredients:

- 1/2 - 2 pounds blueberries
- 1/2 package red wine yeast
- 1/2 tablespoon yeast nutrient
- 1/4 pounds granulated sugar or more
- 1/2 teaspoon pectic enzyme
- 1/4 teaspoon citric acid
- Potassium sorbate, 1/2 teaspoon per gallon
- 8 cups boiled, cooled water

Directions:

1. Place blackberries in a sterilized brew bin and crush the berries using a potato masher or with your hands. Do not over-mash the berries.

2. Add sugar and mix well. Pour water. Stir in yeast nutrient, citric acid and pectic enzyme. Close the lid and place the bin in a cool and dark area for 2 days.

3. Make sure to stir once both days. Place a hydrometer in the mixture and check the gravity. If it shows 1.090, it is fine, else add more sugar until it reaches 1.090. Set aside for another 24 hours.

4. Stir in the red wine yeast. After 6 to 7 days, when active fermentation has stopped, add potassium sorbate.

5. Place a strainer over another sterilized brew bin. Strain the mixture into the bin.

6. Pour the strained mixture into a Demi-John. Seal the bottle and place it in a cool and dark area.

7. After 4 weeks, pour into another Demi-john (do not add the sediments) and place it in a cool and dark area for another 4 weeks.

8. If you are satisfied with the taste, pour into fancy, colored glass bottles, making sure not to add sediments. Go to step 10. Else pour it into a Demi-John bottle set aside for 2 weeks.

9. After 2 weeks, when you are satisfied with the fermentation, pour into fancy colored glass bottles.

10. Put the corks on the bottles.

11. Make sure to label the bottles with the date of preparation and name.

12. Set aside the bottles for 3 – 4 months in a cool and dark area, to mature.

Banana Wine

Preparation Time: 25 Minutes | Cooking Time: 35 Minutes | Servings: 4

Ingredients:

- 1/2 pounds organic bananas, chopped with the peels
- 1/2 cup strong black tea
- 1/4 ounce citric acid
- 1/2 tablespoon yeast nutrient
- 1 pound sugar
- 4 ounces golden raisin, chopped
- 1/2 package white wine yeast
- 4 cups hot water

Directions:

1. Add bananas into a pot along with sugar and mix well.
2. Pour hot water and stir. Place the pot over low heat and cook for about 35 minutes. As it cooks, crush the bananas with the back of a spoon. You can use a potato masher as well.
3. Turn off the heat and let it cool for 10 minutes.
4. Add raisins into a sterilized brew bin.
5. Place a strainer over the bin and strain the banana mixture.
6. Add yeast nutrient, citric acid, white wine yeast, black tea and pectic enzyme into the bin. Stir until well combined. Close the lid and place the bin in a cool and dark area for 5 days.
7. Make sure to stir once on all the days.
8. Place a strainer over another sterilized brew bin. Strain the mixture into the bin.
9. Pour the strained mixture into a Demi-John. Seal the bottle and place it in a cool and dark area.
10. After 4 weeks, pour into another Demi-john (do not add the sediments) and place it in a cool and dark area for 3 – 4 months.
11. If you are satisfied with the taste, pour into fancy, colored glass bottles, making sure not to add sediments. Go to step 13. Else pour it into a Demi-John bottle set aside for 2 weeks.
12. After 2 weeks, when you are satisfied with the fermentation, pour into fancy colored glass bottles.
13. Put the corks on the bottles.
14. Make sure to label the bottles with the date of preparation and name.
15. Set aside the bottles for 3 – 4 months in a cool and dark area, to mature.

Directions:

1. Add water and sugar into a pot and place the pot over medium flame. Boil the water and stir frequently until sugar dissolves.
2. Pour into a sterilized brew bin container. Stir in the cherries. Set aside for 12 hours.
3. Stir in yeast nutrient, citric acid and wine yeast. Close the lid and place the bin in a cool and dark area for 1 day (24 hours).
4. Make sure to stir once. If you think that the mixture is not bubbling, add yeast nutrient from a different package else set aside in a dark place for 7 days. Stir the mixture twice every day.
5. After 6 to 7 days, when active fermentation has stopped, strain and pour into another brew bin. Pour into the Demi-John (do not add the sediments) and place it in a cool and dark area.
6. After 6 – 8 weeks, pour into another Demi-John and place it in a cool and dark area. If you are satisfied with the taste, pour into fancy, colored glass bottles, making sure not to add sediments. Go to step 8. Else pour it into a Demi-John bottle set aside for 2 weeks.
7. After 2 weeks, when you are satisfied with the fermentation, pour into fancy colored glass bottles.
8. Put the corks on the bottles.
9. Make sure to label the bottles with name and date of preparing.
10. Set aside the bottles for 4 – 6 months in a cool and dark area, to mature.

Cherry Wine

Preparation Time: 15 Minutes | Cooking Time:0 | Servings: 4

Ingredients:

- 3 pounds cherries, pitted, stemmed
- 1/2 teaspoon citric acid
- 1/2 tablespoon yeast nutrient
- 1/4 pounds sugar
- 1/2 package red wine yeast
- 4 cups hot water
- Potassium sorbate, 1/2 teaspoon per gallon

Pineapple Wine

Preparation Time: 20 Minutes | Cooking Time: 10 Minutes | Servings: 2

Ingredients:

- 1/2 pounds fresh pineapple, peeled, cored, chopped
- 1/2 tablespoon yeast nutrient
- 1 pound sugar
- 8 ounces golden raisin, chopped
- 1/2 package white wine yeast
- 4 cups hot water

Directions:

1. Add raisins and pineapples into a sterilized brew bin.
2. Add water and sugar into a saucepan and place the saucepan over medium flame. Boil the water and stir frequently until sugar dissolves. Turn off the heat.
3. After 10 minutes, pour into the brew bin, over the pineapple and raisins.
4. Set aside for 12 hours.
5. Stir in yeast nutrient, citric acid and wine yeast. Close the lid and place the bin in a cool and dark area for 1 day (24 hours).
6. Make sure to stir once. If you think that the mixture is not bubbling, add yeast nutrient from a different package else set aside in a dark place for 6 – 7 days, until active fermentation stops. Stir the mixture twice every day.
7. After 6 to 7 days, when active fermentation has stopped, strain and pour into another brew bin. Pour into the Demi-John (do not add the sediments) and place it in a cool and dark area.
8. After 6 – 8 weeks, pour into another Demi-John and place it in a cool and dark area. If you are satisfied with the taste, pour into fancy, colored glass bottles, making sure not to add sediments. Go to step 10. Else pour it into a Demi-John bottle and set aside for 2 weeks.
9. After 2 weeks, when you are satisfied with the fermentation, pour into fancy colored glass bottles.
10. Put the corks on the bottles.
11. Make sure to label the bottles with the date of preparation.
12. Set aside the bottles for 6 – 12 months in a cool and dark area, to mature

Watermelon Wine

Preparation Time: 35 Minutes | Cooking Time:0 | Servings: 4

Ingredients:

- 1/2 large watermelon, chopped into chunks, deseeded, discard green and white part
- 1/2 teaspoon citric acid
- 1/2 teaspoon yeast nutrient
- 1/2 pounds sugar
- 1/4 teaspoon champagne yeast

Directions:

1. Place watermelon in sterilized brew bin containers.

2. Using a potato masher, mash the watermelon. Stir in sugar.
3. Once sugar dissolves, stir in champagne yeast, citric acid and yeast nutrient.
4. Close the lid and place the bin in a cool and dark area for about 12 hours.
5. Place a hydrometer in the mixture and check the gravity. It will be around 1.100.
6. Place the bin in a cool and dark area. Check the gravity every day. The day the hydrometer shows 1.050, place a strainer on another sterilized Demi-John.
7. Place the bottle in a cool and dark area for 3 months.
8. Pour into another Demi-John (do not add the sediments) and place it in a cool and dark area for 2 months.
9. Pour into another Demi-John (do not add sediments) and place it in a cool and dark area for a month.
10. Pour into fancy colored glass bottles.
11. Put the corks on the bottles.
12. Make sure to label the bottles with the date of preparing.
13. Set aside the bottles for 6 – 12 months in a cool and dark area, to mature.

Apple Wine

Preparation Time: 15 Minutes | Cooking Time: 10 Minutes | Servings: 5

Ingredients:

- 3 pounds apples
- 8 ounces golden raisin, chopped
- 1/2 package white wine yeast
- 8 cups hot water
- 1/4 ounce citric acid
- 1/2 tablespoon yeast nutrient
- 1/2 pounds sugar

Directions:

1. Add raisins into a pot
2. Pour hot water and stir. Place the pot over low heat and cook for about 10 minutes.

3. Turn off the heat and let it cool for 10 minutes. Stir in the sugar.
4. Pour the mixture into a sterilized fermenting bin. Core the apples now. Peel and chop the apples right into the bin. Cover the bin. Set aside for 8 hours.
5. Add yeast nutrient, citric acid and white wine yeast into the bin. Stir until well combined. Close the lid and place the bin in a cool and dark area for 5 days.
6. Place a strainer over another bin and strain the apple mixture.
7. Pour into Demi-John. Set aside in a cool and dark area for 3 weeks.
8. Pour the mixture into another Demi-John; make sure not to add the sediments. Seal the bottle and place it in a cool and dark area for 3 weeks.
9. Pour the mixture into another Demi-John; make sure not to add the sediments. Seal the bottle and place it in a cool and dark area for 3 weeks.
10. Pour into fancy colored glass bottles, making sure not to add the sediments.
11. Put the corks on the bottles.
12. Make sure to label the bottles with the date of preparation.
13. Set aside the bottles for 6 – 12 months in a cool and dark area, to mature.

Plum Wine

Preparation Time: 20 Minutes | Cooking Time: 15 Minutes | Servings: 4

Ingredients:

- 2 1/2 pounds pitted plums, chopped
- 1/4 ounce citric acid
- 1/2 tablespoon yeast nutrient
- 1/2 package white wine yeast
- 1/4 pounds granulated sugar
- 1/4 teaspoon pectic enzyme
- 8 cups water

Directions:

1. Place plums in a pot along with sugar and water. Place the pot over medium flame. When

the mixture begins to boil, lower the heat and cook for about 15 minutes. Turn off the heat.

2. Place a strainer over the bin and strain the plum mixture.
3. Add yeast nutrient, citric acid, white wine yeast and pectic enzyme into the bin. Stir until well combined. Close the lid and place the bin in a cool and dark area for 5 days.
4. Place a strainer over another sterilized brew bin. Strain the mixture into the bin, leaving behind the sediments.
5. Pour the strained mixture into a Demi-John. Seal the bottle and place it in a cool and dark area.
6. After 2 weeks, pour into another Demi-john (do not add the sediments) and place it in a cool and dark area for 3 more weeks.
7. Pour into another Demi-john (do not add the sediments) and place it in a cool and dark area for another 3 weeks.
8. Pour into fancy, colored glass bottles, making sure not to add sediments.
9. Put the corks on the bottles.
10. Make sure to label the bottles with the date of preparation and name.
11. The wine is ready to serve.

Elderflower Wine

Preparation Time: 15 Minutes | Cooking Time: 0 | Servings: 2

Ingredients:

- 15 elderflower heads, discard stems
- 1/4 ounce strong black tea
- 1/2 package white wine yeast
- 1/4 ounce citric acid
- 1 pound sugar
- 1/2 ounces sultanas, chopped
- cups boiling hot water
- 2 cups cold water

Directions:

1. Shake the elderflower buds to remove any hidden bugs and add into a sterilized brew bin.
2. Scatter sultanas over the flowers.
3. Pour boiling hot water into a pot. Add sugar and citric acid and stir until sugar dissolves completely.
4. Add it into the bin, all over the flowers. Close the lid and set aside for 12 hours.
5. Add cold water, wine yeast and black tea and stir. Close the lid and keep it in a cool and dark area for 5 days.
6. Place a strainer over another sterilized brew bin. Strain the mixture into the bin, leaving behind the sediments.
7. Pour the strained mixture into a Demi-John. Seal the bottle and place it in a cool and dark area for 6 weeks.
8. Pour into another Demi-john (do not add the sediments) and place it in a cool and dark area for 2 weeks.
9. Pour into fancy, colored glass bottles, making sure not to add sediments.
10. Put the corks on the bottles.
11. Make sure to label the bottles with the date of preparation and name.
12. Place the bottles in a cool and dry area for 4 – 6 months to mature.

Sake (Rice Wine)

Preparation Time: 10 Minutes | Cooking Time: 15 Minutes | Servings: 3

Ingredients:

- 4 cups Thai Jasmine rice, uncooked
- 6 cups water
- 4 Chinese yeast balls

Directions:

1. Pour water into a large saucepan. When water comes to a boil, stir in the rice.
2. Cook covered, on low flame until rice is cooked. Turn off the heat and let the rice cool to about 85 degree F.
3. Meanwhile, place the yeast balls in a plastic bag and crush the balls until it is powdered.
4. Spread some of the rice in the jar. Scatter a little of the yeast over the rice. Repeat this layering of rice and yeast a few times until all of it is added in the jar.
5. Take a large piece of cheesecloth and fold it a few times and cover the top of the jar. Place the lid. Make sure that the lid is not airtight.
6. Set aside on your countertop to ferment for 2 weeks. Stir once every day. The topmost layer of the rice should not be dry so it is necessary to stir daily.
7. Place the nylon bag in a pitcher. Add the fermented rice into the bag and squeeze the bag to remove as much liquid as possible.
8. Pour into bottles. You can serve it now if desired but it will look cloudy. If you want clear wine, place the bottles in the refrigerator for a few days. It will become clearer with time.

Dandelion Wine

Preparation Time: 35 Minutes | Cooking Time: 5 Minutes | Servings: 4

Ingredients:

- 1/2 gallon dandelion flowers, discard the green parts
- Juice of 2 organic oranges
- Zest of 2 organic oranges, grated
- 1/2 gallon boiling water
- 1/2 packet yeast
- 2 pounds cane sugar
- Juice of 2 lemons
- Zest of 2 lemons, grated

Directions:

1. Shake the flowers to dislodge any bugs from the flowers.

2. Place the flowers in the bowl. Pour boiling water over the flowers.
3. Place a strainer over a jar. Pour the flower mixture into the strainer. Discard the flowers.
4. Add lemon juice, orange juice, zests and sugar and stir with a wooden spoon until sugar dissolves completely.
5. Scatter yeast in the jar. Place the lid on the jar, loosely.
6. Place it in a cool and dark area for 2 weeks.
7. Place a strainer over a jar. Pour the mixture into the strainer. Discard the solids
8. Place it in a cool and dark area for 9 months.
9. Pour into fancy, colored glass bottles, making sure not to add sediments.
10. Put the corks on the bottles.
11. Make sure to label the bottles with the date of preparation and name.
12. You can set aside the bottles to mature for a couple of months if desired. This is optional.

Elderberry Wine

Preparation Time: 5 Minutes | Cooking Time: 15 Minutes | Servings: 4

Ingredients:

- 1/2 gallons boiling water

- 1 1/2 gallons black elderberries, remove stems
- 5 pounds cane sugar
- 1/2 packet champagne yeast
- Extra water

Directions:

1. Place elderberries in the brew bin. Pour boiling water into the jar.
2. Keep the bin covered loosely. Let it cool completely (about 8 – 9 hours).
3. Take out a cup of the liquid from the bin and sprinkle yeast over it. Stir well.
4. Add this mixture back into the bin. Mix well.
5. Keep the bin covered loosely. Set aside on your countertop for 3 days. Make sure to stir the mixture 4 hourly.
6. Add sugar into a saucepan. Add little water so that the sugar does not burn.
7. Place the saucepan over medium-low flame. Stir constantly until syrup is formed. Turn off the heat. Cover the saucepan. Let it cool completely.
8. Add the syrup into the brew bin and stir. Close the lid of the jar and set aside to ferment for 5 days.
9. Make sure to stir the mixture 4 hourly.
10. Strain the mixture into the Demi-John. Place the strained berries in a bowl. Add a little water and mash the berries. Strain once again into the Demi-John. Make sure to leave some head space in the jar.
11. Place the fermentation lid. Set aside in a cool and dry area for 9 months.
12. Pour into fancy bottles, leaving behind the sediments. Set aside for 4 – 6 months to mature if desired.

Water Kefir with Fruit Juice

Preparation Time: 5 Minutes | Cooking Time: 15 Minutes | Servings: 5

Ingredients:

- 1/2 cup unrefined cane sugar
- 8 cups water
- 1/4 cup active water kefir grains
- lime, halved
- dried figs

For secondary fermentation: (optional)

- 2 cups fruit juice of your choice

Directions:

1. For initial fermentation: Boil 2 cups of water over high flame. Turn off the heat. Add sugar to the boiled water. Stir until the sugar is completely dissolved. Keep it aside to cool completely.
2. Pour the sugar solution into the jar / jars.
3. Place kefir grains in the jar or divide the grains equally among the smaller jars. Add limes and figs to the large jar or divide among the jars. Cover the jar loosely with a lid or with a cheesecloth such that little air is entering the jar. Keep aside to ferment for 1 - 3 days.
4. Place the strainer over a pitcher and pour the kefir into the strainer. Discard the lime and figs. Retain the kefir grains to make another batch. Place the kefir grains in sugar solution in the refrigerator and use it within 2 weeks.
5. The kefir is now ready to serve. Pour kefir into flip-top bottles and refrigerate until use.
6. If you want to have flavored kefir, proceed to the secondary fermentation.

7. For secondary fermentation: Add fruit juice to the kefir in the previous step (step 5) and transfer into flip-top bottles. Close tightly. Keep aside for 2-3 days on your countertop.

8. Keep the bottles in refrigerator for at least 3 more days before serving. Be careful in opening the bottles while serving as the liquid might ooze out.

9. Note: You can use fresh fruit of your choice instead of fruit juice. The fruits should be ripe. You can use berries, peach, apples, pineapple, nectarine etc. if you are using fresh fruit, place the fruit in a 3rd jar. Muddle the fruits until it releases juice. You can add some whole spices if desired. Pour the ready kefir over the fruit and set aside for 24 hours. Open the lid every 8 hours to release built up gasses.

Milk Kefir

Preparation Time: 5 Minutes | Cooking Time:0 | Servings: 4

Ingredients:

- 2 teaspoons active kefir grains
- 2 cups whole-fat milk

Directions:

1. Place kefir grains in the glass jar. Cover the jar with cheesecloth and fasten it with a rubber band. Do not place the lid.
2. Keep the jar at room temperature for 1 – 2 days. Make sure it is not under sunlight. If the fermentation has not taken place, discard the kefir grains and use new kefir grains.

3. Strain into the storage container using a strainer. It is ready to serve now.
4. Refrigerate the kefir until use. It can last for a week.
5. Place the used kefir grains in a container with fresh milk and refrigerate until use. It can last for a week.

Coconut Water Kefir

Preparation Time: 5 Minutes | Cooking Time:0 | Servings: 4

Ingredients:

- 8 cups coconut water
- 1/2 cup sugar (optional)
- 1/2 cup active water kefir grains

Directions:

1. Combine sugar and coconut water in the jar. Stir until sugar dissolves completely.
2. Drop the kefir grains in the jar.
3. Cover the jar with cheesecloth and fasten it with a rubber band. Do not place the lid.
4. Keep the jar in a warm area for 1 – 2 days. Make sure it is not under sunlight. If the fermentation has not taken place, discard the kefir grains and use new kefir grains. It will take 24 hours to ferment if you are not adding sugar. If you are adding sugar, it will take 48 hours to ferment.
5. Strain into the storage container using a strainer. It is ready to serve now.
6. Refrigerate the kefir until use. It can last for a week.
7. You can add some flavors if desired. For this, the second fermentation process should take place- refer to the Water kefir recipe for 2nd fermentation.

Water Kefir Soda

Preparation Time: 15 Minutes | Cooking Time:0 | Servings: 2

Ingredients:

- 1 gallon water, filtered and without chlorine
- 1/2 cup sugar
- 1/2 cup active water kefir grains
- ounces fruit juice per jar (grape or apple or pomegranate or cherry)

Directions:

1. Add sugar into the jar. Heat about a cup of water and pour into the jar. Stir until sugar dissolves completely.
2. Stir in remaining water. Drop the kefir grains in the jar.
3. Cover the jar with cheesecloth and fasten it with a rubber band. Do not place the lid.
4. Keep the jar in a warm area for 1 – 2 days. Make sure it is not under sunlight.
5. Strain the mixture and pour into 1-quart jars (divide equally). Retain the kefir grains to make another batch. Place the kefir grains in sugar solution in the refrigerator and use it within 2 weeks.
6. Pour 2 ounces fruit juice into each jar. Tighten the lid and shake the jar lightly to mix well.
7. Place on your countertop for 2 days.
8. It is ready to serve now. Chill and serve.
9. It can last for 2 weeks.

Pomegranate Punch Soda

Preparation Time: 5 Minutes | Cooking Time:0 | Servings: 5

Ingredients:

- 3 cups water
- 4 cups pomegranate juice
- 12 tablespoons sugar
- 1/2 cup ginger bug starter

Directions:

1. Add ginger bug, water, sugar and pomegranate juice into the bowl and stir until sugar dissolves completely.
2. Keep the bowl covered with cheesecloth and fasten it with a rubber band.

3. Place the bowl in a warm area, without direct sunlight. Stir the mixture every day.
4. In a couple of days or may be 3 – 4 days, bubbles will be visible when you stir the mixture.
5. Pour into the plastic bottles. Tighten the cap and place it on your countertop for 5 – 7 days.
6. Chill until use.
7. It can last for 3 weeks.

Peaches 'N' Cream Soda

Preparation Time: 10 Minutes | Cooking Time: 15 Minutes | Servings: 2

Ingredients:

- 2 1/2 cups peaches, pitted, sliced
- 3 1/2 cups water
- 1/4 cup liquid whey
- 1/2 cup organic pure cane sugar
- tablespoon vanilla extract

Directions:

1. Add peaches, water and sugar into a pot and stir. Place the pot over medium flame.
2. When it begins to boil, lower the heat and simmer for about 15 minutes. Mash the peaches using a potato masher, while cooking.
3. Place the strainer over a pitcher. Strain the peach mixture into the pitcher.
4. Stir in vanilla extract and whey. Pour into flip-top bottles. Tighten the caps/

5. Place the bottles in a warm place where there is no direct sunlight. Allow it to ferment for 2-7 days. Open the bottles after 2 days to check.
6. Taste and check if you like the taste else ferment it for 3 – 4 days, checking for the taste daily.
7. Place the bottles in the refrigerator until use.
8. It can last for 2 weeks.

Raspberry Soda

Preparation Time: 10 Minutes | Cooking Time: 15 Minutes | Servings: 2

Ingredients:

- 2 cups organic raspberries, fresh or frozen
- 2 – 4 tablespoons liquid whey or water kefir or sauerkraut juice
- 1/2 cup organic sugar or raw honey
- 4 cups water

Directions:

1. Add raspberries and sugar into a pot and stir. Place the pot over medium flame.
2. When it begins to boil, lower the heat and simmer for about 15 minutes. Mash the raspberries using a potato masher, while cooking.
3. Place the strainer over a fermentation bin. Strain the raspberry mixture into the bin.
4. Stir in water and whey. Cover the bin with fermentation lids. Set aside in a cool and dark area for 2 – 3 days. Pour into flip-top bottles. Tighten the caps.
5. Place the bottles in the refrigerator until use. Let it chill for at least 24 hours before serving.
6. It can last for 2 weeks.

Orange Soda

Preparation Time: 10 Minutes | Cooking Time: 15 Minutes | Servings: 2

Ingredients:

- 2 cups organic cane sugar
- 2 1/2 cups fresh orange juice

- 12 cups water
- cup liquid whey

Directions:

1. Combine 6 cups of water and sugar in a large pot. Place the pot over medium flame and stir frequently. When sugar has dissolved completely, turn off the heat.
2. Stir in 6 cups water, orange juice and whey.
3. Pour the mixture into flip-top bottles. Keep the bottles in a warm place for about 3 days or until you are satisfied with the fermentation.
4. Chill until use.
5. It can last for 2 weeks.

Grape Soda

Preparation Time: 5 Minutes | Cooking Time: 0 | Servings: 1

Ingredients:

- 1/4 cup ginger bug starter

- 1 1/2 pounds red seedless grapes

Directions:

1. Blend the grapes in a blender until very smooth.
2. Place a strainer over the bowl. Pour the blended juice into the strainer. Press the solids to remove as much juice as possible. You should have around 2 cups of juice.
3. Add ginger bug into the bowl and stir well. Keep the bowl covered with cheesecloth and fasten it with a rubber band.
4. Place the bowl in a warm area, without direct sunlight. Remove the white scum like thing that will be floating on top, from time to time. In a couple of days or may be 3 – 4 days, bubbles will be visible when you stir the mixture.
5. Now strain into the plastic bottle. Tighten the cap and place it for one more day on your countertop.
6. Chill until use.
7. It can last for 2 weeks.

Strawberry Soda

Preparation Time: 10 Minutes | Cooking Time: 30 Minutes | Servings: 2

Ingredients:

- 4 cups filtered water
- 1/2 cup ginger bug
- 1/2 pound strawberries
- 3/4 cup dehydrated cane juice

Directions:

1. To make wort: Take a large, square piece of cheesecloth and place the strawberries on it. Bring all the edges of the cloth together and tie it tightly with twine that is used in cooking, with some extra twine to hang it on the pot.
2. Place a heavy bottomed pot over medium heat. Pour water in it.
3. Tie the cheesecloth bag to the handle of the pot with the extra twine and drop the bag in the pot, it should immerse in the water.
4. When the water begins to boil, lower the heat and cook covered for 20-30 minutes.

5. Stir in the sugar. Once sugar is completely dissolved, turn off the heat. Let the pot rest for about 30minutes. The pot should be covered while resting.
6. Remove the strawberry cheesecloth bag. Let the strawberry wort cool to room temperature.
7. Add ginger bug liquid and stir until well combined. Pour the mixture into bottles with lids tightly fastened.
8. For fermenting: Place the jar at room temperature. Make sure that there is no sunlight falling on the bottles. Set the bottles aside on your countertop for 2 days.
9. Place in the refrigerator until use.
10. It can last for 3 weeks.

Apple Soda

Preparation Time: 5 Minutes | Cooking Time:0 | Servings: 4

Ingredients:

- 1/4 cup ginger bug starter
- 2 cups unpasteurized apple juice
- teaspoon apple pie spice

Directions:

1. Add ginger bug, apple pie spice and apple juice into the bowl and stir well. Keep the bowl covered with cheesecloth and fasten it with a rubber band.
2. Place the bowl in a warm area, without direct sunlight. Remove the white scum like thing that will be floating on top, from time to time. In a couple of days or may be 3 – 4 days, bubbles will be visible when you stir the mixture.

3. Strain the mixture and pour into the plastic bottle. Tighten the cap and place it for one more day on your countertop.
4. Chill until use.
5. It can last for 3 weeks.

Tea Ginger Soda Pop

Preparation Time: 15 Minutes | Cooking Time:0 | Servings: 3

Ingredients:

- 7 cups brewed black tea or green tea, cooled
- 12 tablespoons sugar
- inch piece ginger, peeled, minced
- 1/2 cup ginger bug starter

Directions:

1. Add ginger bug, ginger, sugar and tea into the bowl and stir until sugar dissolves completely.
2. Keep the bowl covered with cheesecloth and fasten it with a rubber band.
3. Place the bowl in a warm area, without direct sunlight for 3 – 4 days. Stir the mixture every day.
4. In a couple of days or may be 3 – 4 days, bubbles will be visible when you stir the mixture.
5. Strain the mixture and pour into the plastic bottles. Tighten the cap and place it on your countertop for 5 – 7 days.
6. Chill until use.
7. It can last for 3 weeks.

Cranberry Soda (Immunity Booster)

Preparation Time: 15 Minutes | Cooking Time:0 | Servings: 2

Ingredients:

- 6 cups water
- cup cranberry juice
- 1/4 cup grated, fresh turmeric
- Juice of 2 lemons
- Zest of 2 lemons, grated

- 12 tablespoons sugar
- 1/2 cup ginger bug starter

Directions:

1. Add ginger bug, water, sugar, lemon juice, turmeric, lemon zest and cranberry juice into the bowl and stir until sugar dissolves completely.
2. Keep the bowl covered with cheesecloth and fasten it with a rubber band.
3. Place the bowl in a warm area, without direct sunlight for 3 – 4 days. Stir the mixture every day.
4. In a couple of days or may be 3 – 4 days, bubbles will be visible when you stir the mixture.
5. Strain the mixture and pour into the plastic bottles. Tighten the cap and place it on your countertop for 4 – 5 days.
6. Chill until use.
7. It can last for 3 weeks.

Blueberry Soda

Preparation Time: 5 Minutes | Cooking Time: 20 Minutes | Servings: 4

Ingredients:

- 2 cups organic blueberries, fresh or frozen
- 4 tablespoons liquid whey
- 1/2 cup organic sugar or dehydrated cane juice or rapadura
- 4 cups filtered water

Directions:

1. Add blueberries and sugar into a pot and stir. Place the pot over medium flame.
2. When it begins to boil, lower the heat and simmer for about 20 minutes. Mash the blueberries using a potato masher, while cooking.
3. Place the strainer over a fermentation bin. Strain the raspberry mixture into the bin.
4. Stir in water and whey. Cover the bin with fermentation lids. Set aside in a cool and dark area for 2 – 3 days. Pour into flip-top bottles. Tighten the cap of the bottles.

5. Place the bottles in the refrigerator until use. Let it chill for at least 24 hours before serving.
6. It can last for 2 weeks.

Vanilla Cream Soda

Preparation Time: 15 Minutes | Cooking Time:0 | Servings: 2

Ingredients:

- cup prunes
- 4 tablespoons kombucha
- 1/4 cup organic sugar or dehydrated cane juice or rapadura
- 4 – 5 tablespoons vanilla syrup
- 4 cups filtered water

Directions:

1. Add prunes, water and sugar into a brew bin and stir until sugar dissolves completely.
2. Stir in kombucha and vanilla syrup. Cover the bin with fermentation lids. Set aside in a cool and dark area for 2 – 3 days. Pour into flip-top bottles. Tighten the cap of the bottles. Place on your countertop for 2 – 3 days or until you are satisfied with the fermentation.
3. Place the bottles in the refrigerator until use. Let it chill for at least 24 hours before serving.
4. It can last for 2 weeks.

Turmeric Bug Sodas

Preparation Time: 15 Minutes | Cooking Time:0 | Servings: 2

Ingredients:

- 7 cups water
- 1/2 cup turmeric bug starter
- 6 – 12 tablespoons sugar
- 1/2 cup finely grated fresh turmeric

Directions:

1. Add water, turmeric bug, sugar and fresh turmeric into the jar. Stir until sugar dissolves completely.

2. Cover the jar with cheesecloth and fasten with a rubber band.
3. Keep the jar in a warm and dark area where there isn't sunlight falling on the jar.
4. Bubbles should be visible around the 3rd day through fermentation.
5. When bubbles are visible, pour the mixture into bottles after straining.
6. Place the bottles in a cool and dark area for 10 – 15 days.
7. Refrigerate until use. Use within a month

Lemonade Soda

Preparation Time: 15 Minutes | Cooking Time:0 | Servings: 3

Ingredients:

- 6 cups water
- cup lemon juice
- Zest of 4 lemons, grated
- 12 tablespoons sugar
- 1/2 cup ginger bug starter

Directions:

1. Add ginger bug, water, sugar, lemon juice and lemon zest into the bowl and stir until sugar dissolves completely.
2. Keep the bowl covered with cheesecloth and fasten it with a rubber band.
3. Place the bowl in a warm area, without direct sunlight for 3 – 4 days. Stir the mixture every day.
4. In a couple of days or may be 3 – 4 days, bubbles will be visible when you stir the mixture.
5. Strain the mixture and pour into the plastic bottles. Tighten the cap and place it on your countertop for 4 – 5 days.
6. Chill until use.

Mango Beer

Preparation Time: 10 Minutes | Cooking Time:0 | Servings: 4

Ingredients:

- pounds fresh, overripe mangoes
- teaspoon fruit ale yeast
- 0.018 ounce potassium meta bi sulphite
- 1/2 teaspoon ground ginger or to taste
- 1/2 tablespoon gelatin
- pounds dry malt extract
- 0.035 ounce pectic enzyme
- 1 tablespoon sugar
- 0.05 ounce bentonite
- Herbs of your choice (optional)
- Boiled, cooled and chilled water, as required

Directions:

1. Remove pulp from the mangoes. Rinse the skin of the mangoes and the stones in 2-1/2 quarts water and use the water to make wort.
2. Make a solution of potassium Meta bi sulphite and place it in an airtight jar along with mango pulp and pectic enzyme. Mix well. Set aside for 24 hours.
3. To make wort: Add mango rinsed water into a pot and place the pot over medium flame. Stirring constantly, add dry malt extract. Keep stirring else you will end up with lumps.
4. Stir in ground ginger and herbs if using and remove the pot from heat.
5. Stir in mango pulp. Pour enough boiled and chilled water such that the mixture is 5 quarts.
6. Transfer the mixture into the brew bin. Add half the fruit ale yeast and stir. Also add bentonite solution and stir.
7. Close the bin with fermentation lids. Set aside in a dry area for 4 days. Check for active fermentation. If active fermentation has stopped, go to step 8 else keep the bin aside for one more day.

8. Taste and add sweetener if desired.
9. Stir in gelatin and set aside for a day.
10. Combine priming sugar and remaining yeast in a bowl.
11. Pour the beer into the storage container, after straining. Stir in priming sugar mixture. Place the container in a cool and dry area for 3 days.
12. Chill and serve.

Pineapple Beer

Preparation Time: 10 Minutes | Cooking Time:0 | Servings: 2

Ingredients:

- pineapple, peeled, chop the peels as well as the pulp
- 1/2 cups white sugar
- 1 1/4 teaspoons instant dry yeast
- 12 cups lukewarm water
- 1/2 cup raisins, slightly smashed

Directions:

1. Add pineapple peel, pulp, sugar, raisins and lukewarm water into the fermentation brew bin.
2. Scatter yeast on top and let it sit for a minute, undisturbed.
3. After a minute, mix until well combined.
4. Cover the bin with tulle fabric. Set aside on your countertop for 3 days. Stir it once in the

morning and once in the evening on all the 3 days.

5. Strain the beer and pour into storage containers. Fasten the cap of the containers after 12 hours.
6. Chill until use.

Ginger Beer

Preparation Time: 5 Minutes!Cooking Time: 60 Minutes | Servings: 4

Ingredients:

- 2 quarts filtered water or well water, at room temperature or slightly lukewarm
- 1/4 cup fresh lemon juice
- 10 tablespoons organic cane sugar
- 1/2 cup ginger bug starter
- 3 tablespoons freshly grated ginger

Directions:

1. Add ginger bug, water (make sure not to use tap water), sugar, ginger and lemon juice into the fermentation brew bin and stir until sugar dissolves completely.
2. Keep the bowl covered with cheesecloth and fasten it with a rubber band.
3. Place the bowl in a cool and dark area for 8 – 10 days. Stir the mixture 2 times, every day. After 5 – 6 days, taste it every 2 days to check for sweetness. Add 1 – 2 tablespoons of sugar (only if necessary and do not add more than this amount at a time) and stir.
4. In a few days, white foamy kind of thing surrounding the ginger and bubbles will be visible when you stir the mixture.
5. Taste and check for sweetness. Add 1 – 2 tablespoons if required (only if it does not taste sweet) and a little more ginger
6. Pour into storage containers. Tighten the cap and place it in the refrigerator.
7. Chill until use.

Root Beer

Preparation Time: 5 Minutes | Cooking Time: 25 Minutes | Servings: 4

Ingredients:

- 1/4 cup sassafras root bark
- 1/2 cup unrefined, organic cane sugar (such as rapadura)
- 1 inch stick cinnamon
- 1 1/2 quarts filtered water
- 6 tablespoons ginger bug or whey
- 1/4 teaspoon wintergreen leaf
- tablespoons molasses
- A pinch ground coriander (optional)
- A pinch allspice (optional)
- tablespoons lime juice (optional but recommended)
- 1 teaspoon pure vanilla extract

Directions:

1. Combine water, sassafras root bark, wintergreen leaves, cinnamon, allspice and coriander in a pot.
2. Place the pot over high flame. When it begins to boil, lower the heat and simmer for 12 – 15 minutes.
3. Strain the mixture into a pitcher using the strainer. Let it cool for 10 minutes.
4. Stir in sugar and molasses. Once it dissolves completely, set it aside for some more time to cool.
5. When the mixture is warm stir in lime juice. Once it is well combined, stir in ginger bug.
6. Pour into bottles. Fasten the cap and set aside to ferment, at room temperature.
7. After 2 days, check out if it is fermented to suit your taste. If you are satisfied, place the bottles in the refrigerator else let it ferment until it gets the taste you desire.

Belgium Wild Beer

Preparation Time: 5 Minutes | Cooking Time: 20 Minutes | Servings: 4

Ingredients:

- 64 ounces water
- ounce common yarrow
- 0.15 ounce chopped, dried dandelion roots
- ounce wormwood

- 0.25 ounce fresh ground ivy
- – 3 crushed stems (4 inches each) bitter dock or juice of a lemon
- 1/2 teaspoons yeast
- 12 ounces brown sugar
- Extra brown sugar for the bottles

Directions:

1. Combine brown sugar, water, wormwood, dandelion, yarrow and bitter dock stems or lemon in a pot.
2. Place the pot over medium flame. When it begins to boil, lower the heat and simmer for about 20 minutes.
3. Stir in ground ivy after about 12 – 15 minutes of simmering. Turn off the heat after adding ground ivy.
4. Strain the mixture into the brew bin. Add yeast. Close the lid and set aside for 10 days.
5. Pour into flip top bottles. Add 1/2 teaspoon brown sugar into each bottle. Fasten the lid and store in a dry area for about 3 weeks.
6. The beer is now ready to serve.
7. Chill until use.

Fermented Plum Brandy

Preparation Time: 5 Minutes | Cooking Time: 0 | Servings: 4

Ingredients:

- 2 pounds ripe plums, pitted, sliced
- Brandy, as required
- cup sugar

Directions:

1. Add plum and sugar in the glass jar and stir until the plum is well coated with the sugar.
2. Close the jar with the fermentation lid. Place the jar aside for 2 weeks, at room temperature.
3. Strain the juice and measure it. Add equal quantities of brandy (as much as the measured juice) and pour into bottles.
4. Chill until use. It can last for a month.

Elderflower Champagne

Preparation Time: 5 Minutes | Cooking Time: 0 | Servings: 4

Ingredients:

- 3 – 4 large elderflowers or 6 – 8 clusters of small elderflowers, do not rinse, discard tough stalks
- 6 cups cold, filtered water
- 2 tablespoons cider vinegar
- 2 cups filtered boiling water
- 1/2 pound honey or 3/4 pound sugar

Directions:

1. Shake the elderflowers to remove any bugs that may be hidden.
2. Add honey or sugar into a bowl. Pour boiling water over it and stir until sugar dissolves completely. The fermentation process by using honey will take longer than by using sugar.
3. Add cold water, elderberry flowers and vinegar and mix well.
4. Cover the bowl with a kitchen towel and place it on your countertop for 2 days. Stir 2 – 3 times on each day.
5. Few bubbles in the mixture should be visible when you are done by the end of 2 days. If you do not see bubbles, add a very tiny pinch of baking yeast and cover it again. Set aside for another 2 days, stirring 2 – 3 times daily.
6. Strain the mixture into a pitcher and discard the solids. Pour the mixture into bottles. Do not fill up to the top. Leave about an inch space below the neck of the bottle.

7. Place the bottles on your countertop for 6 – 7 days. Open the bottle once every day for a few seconds and close it again.
8. When you are satisfied with the taste, shift the bottles into the refrigerator until use.

Fruit Kvass with Apple and Raspberries

Preparation Time: 5 Minutes | Cooking Time:0 | Servings: 4

Ingredients:

- 4 organic apples, cored, sliced
- cup raspberries
- tablespoons honey (optional)
- teaspoons grated fresh ginger
- 1 cup whey liquid
- Water, as required

Directions:

1. Add apples, raspberries, honey, ginger and whey into a 2 quart jar. Pour enough water to fill the jar. Leave about 2 inches from the top. Tighten the lid.
2. Place the jar at room temperature without any sunlight falling on the jar. Let it ferment for 2-3 days. Shake the jar 2-3 times every day.
3. Open the lid every other day. Push the fruits down and close the lid tightly again. When the kvass is ready, lots of bubbles will be visible in the jar. The kvass is ready when it has a pleasant taste or the taste you prefer is achieved.
4. Strain and pour into bottles with a plastic lid.
5. Place in the refrigerator until use.
6. To serve: Dilute with chilled water and serve.

Fruit Kvass with Peach and Blackberries

Preparation Time: 5 Minutes | Cooking Time:0 | Servings: 4

Ingredients:

- 1/8 jar ripe fresh peaches
- 1/8 jar blackberries
- 1/2 inch fresh ginger, peeled

- 1/2 tablespoon raw honey
- Purified water or filtered water, as required

Directions:

1. Add peaches, blackberries, ginger and honey into the jar. Pour enough water to fill up the jar, leaving about 2 inches space on top.
2. Fasten the lid of the jar and keep it on your countertop, at room temperature for 2 to 3 days, shaking the jar 2 – 3 times.
3. The day bubbles are visible; unscrew the lid to release some air. If there seems no fermentation even after 2 to 3 days, it is advisable to add whey or yeast to speed up the fermentation. You can also use kombucha.
4. Strain the mixture into a pitcher and pour into storage bottles.
5. Place the bottles on your countertop for a couple of days if desired.
6. Refrigerate until use. It can last for a week.

Apple Kvass

Preparation Time: 5 Minutes | Cooking Time: 5 Minutes | Servings: 4

Ingredients:

- 2 quarts water
- ounces sugar
- 0.5 ounce yeast
- pounds Antonov apples or any apples that have high tannin
- ounces honey
- 1/2 teaspoon ground cinnamon

Directions:

1. Add water and apples into a saucepan. Place the saucepan over medium heat.
2. When the mixture comes to a boil, turn off the heat. Set aside the mixture for about 3 hours.
3. Strain the mixture into a jar. Stir in honey, sugar, cinnamon and yeast. Tighten the lid and keep it in a warm place for 2 – 3 days.
4. Strain the mixture and pour into bottles. Refrigerate for 3 – 4 days before using.
5. It can last for about 5 days (after chilling for 4 days before using).

Fruit Kvass with Cherries and Raspberries

Preparation Time: 5 Minutes | Cooking Time:0 | Servings: 4

Ingredients:

- 1/8 jar ripe fresh cherries
- 1/8 jar fresh raspberries
- 2 pods cardamom
- 1/2 tablespoon raw honey
- Purified water or filtered water, as required

Directions:

1. Add cherries, raspberries, cardamom and honey into the jar. Pour enough water to fill up the jar, leaving about 2 inches space on top.
2. Fasten the lid of the jar and keep it on your countertop, at room temperature for 2 to 3 days, shaking the jar 2 – 3 times.
3. The day bubbles are visible; unscrew the lid to release some air. If there seems no fermentation even after 2 to 3 days, it is advisable to add whey or yeast to speed up the fermentation. You can also use kombucha.
4. Strain the mixture into a pitcher and pour into storage bottles.
5. Place the bottles on your countertop for a couple of days if desired.
6. Refrigerate until use. It can last for a week.

Fruit Kvass with Lemon, Apricot and Ginger

Preparation Time: 15 Minutes | Cooking Time:0 | Servings: 4

Ingredients:

- 2 cups chopped dried apricots
- 5 – 6 lemons, sliced
- 1/2 inch fresh ginger, peeled
- 1/2 tablespoon raw honey
- Purified water or filtered water, as required

Directions:

1. Add apricots, lemon, ginger and honey into the jar. Pour enough water to fill up the jar, leaving about 2 inches space on top.
2. Fasten the lid of the jar and keep it on your countertop, at room temperature for 2 to 3 days, shaking the jar 2 – 3 times.
3. The day bubbles are visible; unscrew the lid to release some air. If there seems no fermentation even after 2 to 3 days, it is advisable to add whey or yeast to speed up the fermentation. You can also use kombucha.
4. Strain the mixture into a pitcher and pour into storage bottles.
5. Place the bottles on your countertop for a couple of days if desired.
6. Refrigerate until use. It can last for a week.

Lemon-Mint Kvass

Preparation Time: 5 Minutes | Cooking Time: 60 Minutes | Servings: 4

Ingredients:

- 2 quarts water
- 1/2 tablespoons sugar
- Juice of a lemon
- Zest of a lemon, chopped
- ounces rhubarb, chopped
- 4 tablespoons honey
- A handful fresh mint leaves
- tablespoons currants

Directions:

1. Add water and rhubarb into a saucepan. Place the saucepan over medium heat.
2. When the mixture comes to a boil, turn off the heat. Set aside the mixture until the temperature of the mixture is about 60 to 7o degree F.
3. Pour the mixture into a jar. Stir in honey, sugar, mint, lemon zest, lemon juice and currants. Stir until honey and sugar are dissolved completely.
4. Tighten the lid and keep it in a warm place for 1 day.
5. Strain the mixture and pour into bottles. Place the bottles in a cool and dry area.
6. Chill and serve. It can last for a week.

Cranberry or Lingonberry Kvass

Preparation Time: 5 Minutes | Cooking Time: 20 Minutes | Servings: 2

Ingredients:

- pounds cranberries or lingonberries
- 2 quarts water
- 1/2 tablespoons sugar
- 0.18 ounce yeast
- 1 lemon, sliced

Directions:

1. Add water and the berries into a saucepan. Set aside for 20 minutes.
2. Mash the berries well to squeeze out as much juice as possible.
3. Place the saucepan over medium heat.

4. When the mixture comes to a boil, turn off the heat. Set aside the mixture until it cools completely.
5. Pour the mixture into a jar. Stir in sugar, lemon slices and yeast. Stir until sugar dissolves completely.
6. Tighten the lid and keep it aside for 16 hours.
7. Strain the mixture and pour into bottles. Place the bottles in the refrigerator.
8. Chill and serve. It can last for a week.

Black Raspberry Kvass

Preparation Time: 25 Minutes | Cooking Time:0 | Servings: 4

Ingredients:

- 2 cups black raspberries
- 1/2 cup whey liquid
- 2 tablespoons raw honey
- 2 quarts purified water or filtered water

Directions:

1. Add raspberries, water and honey into the jar. Stir until honey dissolves completely.
2. Fasten the lid of the jar and keep it on your countertop, at room temperature for 2 to 3 days, shaking the jar 2 – 3 times.
3. The day bubbles are visible; unscrew the lid to release some air. If there seems no fermentation even after 2 to 3 days.
4. Strain the mixture into a pitcher and pour into storage bottles.
5. Refrigerate until use. It can last for a week.

Mango Kvass

Preparation Time: 15 Minutes | Cooking Time:0 | Servings: 6

Ingredients:

- 2 quarts water
- ounces sugar
- 0.5 ounce yeast
- pounds mangoes, peeled, chopped
- ounces honey

- 2 teaspoons chai spices

Directions:

1. Add mango and water into a jar. Stir in honey, chai spices and yeast. Tighten the lid and keep it in a warm place for 2 – 3 days.
2. Strain the mixture into a pitcher and pour into bottles.
3. Refrigerate until use. It can last for a week.

Pulque

Preparation Time: 5 Minutes | Cooking Time: 15 Minutes | Servings: 6

Ingredients:

- 4 ounces coriander seeds, crushed
- 1/2 pound champagne yeast
- 4 pounds dark agave nectar
- 2 gallons spring water

Directions:

1. Make sure that the yeast is primed a day before brewing pulque.
2. Pour water into the pot and place the pot over high flame. When it starts boiling, turn off the heat.
3. Stir coriander and agave nectar into the water. Place the pot once again over medium flame.
4. Stir constantly for about 15 – 18 minutes. Turn off the heat and cool completely.
5. Transfer the mixture into the brew bin. Add champagne yeast and stir. Close the lid and set aside for 2 – 3 weeks.
6. Transfer into another brew bin and set aside for a week.
7. Strain into a pitcher.
8. Refrigerate until use. It can last for 2 weeks.
9. Serve with ice and lemon slices.

Kombucha Tea

Preparation Time: 5 Minutes | Cooking Time: 15 Minutes | Servings: 6

Ingredients:

- 3/4 quarts water
- 4 black tea bags or green tea bags or a 2 green tea bags and 2 black tea bags or 1 tablespoon loose tea
- 1 scoby for each fermentation jar
- 1/2 cup granulated sugar
- 1 cup starter tea from last batch of kombucha tea or store bought kombucha (unpasteurized, neutral flavored)
- Optional flavoring for bottling: Use any one or more
- 1/2 - 1 cup chopped fruits of your choice
- 1 tablespoon flavored tea of your choice
- 1-2 tablespoons fresh herbs or spices
- 1-2 cups fruit juice
- tablespoons honey

Directions:

1. To make tea base: Boil water in the stockpot. Turn off the heat.
2. Add sugar and stir until it dissolves completely. Add the tea bags or loose tea. Let the tea infuse until the water has cooled completely.
3. Discard the tea bags. Strain the tea if using tea leaves.
4. Add starter tea and stir until well combined.
5. Pour into the glass jars. Carefully add the scoby into the jar. Make sure that your hands are clean and dry.
6. Place layers of tightly woven cloth at the m the jar. You can also cover with coffee filters. You can also use paper towels.
7. Fasten with a rubber band.
8. Place the jar at room temperature for 7 – 10 days. Make sure that there is no sunlight falling on the jar.
9. Keep a check on the kombucha and scoby every other day initially and after 5-6 days, check it daily.
10. The scoby generally tends to float at the top or bottom or sideways. A new scoby will begin to form on the surface of the kombucha. It should be cream in color. It generally tends to attach to the old scoby.
11. In a few days through fermentation, you will begin to see bubbles in the jar around the scoby especially. You may also see some sedimentation at the bottom of the jar. It's perfectly normal.

12. Taste a little of the kombucha daily, after 7 days. When you find the taste is pleasant, your kombucha is ready. It should have a sweet as well as pungent sour taste.
13. Remove the scoby. Remove some of this kombucha tea and use it as a starter for the next batch of kombucha tea.
14. If you are using any of the optional flavorings, add them to the glass jar. Set aside the jar for a day for the flavors to infuse. Keep the jar covered.
15. Pour the kombucha tea into bottles.
16. Place the bottled kombucha at room temperature for 1-3 days, without any sunlight falling over the bottles.
17. Shift the bottles into the refrigerator.
18. Use within a month.

Apple Cinnamon Kombucha

Preparation Time: 15 Minutes | Cooking Time:0 | Servings: 2

Ingredients:

- 1/2 medium apple, diced or use 1/3 cup apple juice
- Kombucha, as required
- teaspoon cinnamon chips

Directions:

1. Place apples and cinnamon into the jar. Pour enough kombucha to fill up the jar.

2. Fasten the lid and place on your countertop for 3 – 7 days.
3. Strain and pour into storage bottles.
4. Refrigerate untie.

Sparkling Bubble Tea

Preparation Time: 5 Minutes | Cooking Time:0 | Servings: 1

Ingredients:

- 4 tablespoons chia seeds
- quart kombucha

Directions:

1. Add kombucha and chia seeds into the jar
2. Fasten the lid and place on your countertop for 2 – 3 days.
3. Refrigerate until use.

Citrus Tea

Preparation Time: 15 Minutes | Cooking Time:0 | Servings: 1

Ingredients:

- lemon, sliced
- 1 lime, sliced
- 1 orange, sliced
- 1/4 grapefruit, sliced
- Kombucha, as required

Directions:

1. Slice the citrus fruits along with the peel and place in the jar. Pour enough kombucha to fill up the jar.
2. Fasten the lid and place on your countertop for 2 – 3 days or until you are satisfied with the fermentation.
3. Strain and pour into storage bottles.
4. Refrigerate until use.

Peach Pie Kombucha

Preparation Time: 15 Minutes | Cooking Time:0 | Servings: 2

Ingredients:

- quart kombucha
- 1 tablespoon maple syrup
- 1/2 ripe peach, pitted, finely chopped
- 1/4 teaspoon vanilla, divided

Directions:

1. Add kombucha, maple syrup, peach and vanilla into the jar and stir well.
2. Fasten the lid and place on your countertop for 3 – 10 days, depending on how much you want it fermented.
3. Strain the mixture into a pitcher. Discard the solids and pour strained liquid back into the jar.
4. Refrigerate until use.

Rosemary Grape Kombucha

Preparation Time: 15 Minutes | Cooking Time:0 | Servings: 2

Ingredients:

- quart kombucha
- 1 sprig rosemary
- 1/2 cup red grapes or 1/4 cup grape juice

Directions:

1. Blend the grapes in a blender until smooth.
2. Add kombucha, rosemary and grape juice into the jar. Stir well.
3. Fasten the lid and place on your countertop for 3 – 10 days depending on how much you want it fermented.
4. Refrigerate until use.
5. Strain the mixture into a pitcher just before serving. Discard the solids and serve.
6. It can last for 4 – 5 weeks.

Turmeric Kombucha

Preparation Time: 15 Minutes | Cooking Time:0 | Servings: 4

Ingredients:

- quart kombucha
- 1/8 teaspoon ground cinnamon or 1 teaspoon grated ginger
- 1/4 teaspoon turmeric powder or 1 teaspoon fresh grated turmeric
- 1 teaspoon honey or 2 tablespoons carrot juice

Directions:

1. Add kombucha, turmeric, cinnamon and honey into the jar. Stir well.
2. Fasten the lid and place on your countertop for 3 – 10 days depending on how much you want it fermented.
3. Refrigerate until use.
4. Strain the mixture if desired.
5. It can last for 4 – 5 weeks.

Bonfire Cider (The Natural Flu Remedy)

Preparation Time: 25 Minutes | Cooking Time:0 | Servings: 8

Ingredients:

- cup peeled, sliced fresh ginger
- 1 cup peeled, sliced horseradish root (optional)
- heads garlic, peeled, sliced
- tablespoons Echinacea root (optional)

- 2 organic lemons, sliced
- sticks cinnamon
- 10 ounces raw apple cider vinegar (ACV)
- 1 cup peeled, sliced fresh turmeric root
- 1 white onion, chopped
- 2 jalapeño peppers, sliced
- 2 sprigs fresh rosemary
- Raw honey to taste

Directions:

1. Add ginger, horseradish, lemon slices, cinnamon, turmeric, onion, jalapeño and rosemary into a Mason's jar. Press it well.
2. Pour apple cider vinegar over it. The vinegar should completely cover all the ingredients in the jar. So add more ACV if required.
3. Place a piece of parchment paper on the top of the jar (on the rim) and close the lid tightly.
4. Place in a warm place, without any sunlight falling on the jar, for about a month.
5. Strain the mixture and discard the solids. Pour the strained mixture into another jar. Add honey and stir until well combined.
6. Refrigerate until use. It can last for about 3 to 4 months.
7. Take a teaspoon of it when you are down with the flu. You can also add it to soups or smoothies to increase your immunity.

Rejuvelac

Preparation Time: 15 Minutes | Cooking Time: 8 – 9 hours | Servings: 2

Ingredients:

- 2 quarts water
- cup wheat berries

Directions:

1. To sprout wheat berries: Soak the wheat berries in water, in the sprouting jar for about 8 – 9 hours.
2. Cover the jar with a mesh sprouting lid.
3. Drain off the water from the jar and rinse well.
4. Set aside to sprout. Rinse a couple of times every day until the sprouts are visible. It should take 2 – 3 days.

5. Drain well and use. Store unused, sprouted wheat berries in an airtight container in the refrigerator. It can last for 3 to 4 days.
6. To make rejuvelac: Add wheat berries and water into a jar. Close the lid and keep it in a warm area for 1 – 2 days, making sure there is no sunlight falling on the jar. When the drink is ready, it will have a little fizz in it and the liquid will look cloudy.
7. Pour only the liquid into bottles and refrigerate until use.
8. It can last for a week.
9. The same used wheat berries can be used to make another batch but use it within 24 hours.

Natural Ginger Ale

Preparation Time: 15 Minutes | Cooking Time: 30 Minutes | Servings: 3

Ingredients:

- 1/2 - 1 inch piece fresh ginger, peeled, minced, or use more to suit your taste
- 1/4 cup fresh lemon juice or lime juice
- 4 cups non-chlorinated filtered water

- 1/4 cup organic sugar or Rapadura or plain sugar mixed with 1/2 tablespoon molasses
- 1/4 teaspoon sea salt or Himalayan salt
- 1/4 cup ginger bug

Directions:

1. For wort: Combine 1 1/2 cups water, salt, ginger, sugar in a saucepan.
2. Place the saucepan over medium flame. Stir occasionally until it comes to a boil.
3. Cook on low heat until the sugar is completely dissolved and the solution has the fragrance of ginger. Turn off the heat.
4. Add remaining water and stir. The mixture should cool completely. If it does not cool completely, set it aside until it cools.
5. Once it cools completely stir in lemon juice and ginger bug. Close the lid of the jar tightly.
6. Place the jar at room temperature for 2-3 days making sure that there is no sunlight falling on the jar. When you open the lid, the liquid should be slightly fizzy with bubbles all over and the fragrance of ginger. You may also hear a hissing sound.
7. Strain and pour the ginger ale into the storage bottles.
8. Refrigerate until use.

Turkish Boza

Preparation Time: 5 Minutes | Cooking Time: 15 Minutes | Servings: 4

Ingredients:

- 2 cups bulgur
- teaspoon vanilla extract
- 1 cup warm water
- Filtered water, as required
- 1 3/4 cups sugar, divided
- 1/2 ounce yeast

To serve:

- Ground cinnamon
- A handful roasted chickpeas

Directions:

1. Place bulgur in a pan. Pour enough water to cover the bulgur. The water should be at least 2 – 3 inches over the bulgur.
2. Add more water into the pan. Place the pan over low flame and cook until soft. It can take a couple of hours. Stir frequently. Turn off the heat.
3. Place a strainer over a bowl. Add a little of the cooked bulgur into the strainer. Press the bulgur with the back of a spoon to remove as much liquid as possible. Press well. Discard the pressed bulgur.
4. Repeat the previous step a few times, adding a little of the cooked bulgur each time.
5. Add sugar, yeast and warm water into another bowl and stir well. Set aside for 10 minutes. Pour this mixture into the bowl of pressed liquid. Stir well.
6. Cover the bowl with cheesecloth and set aside on your countertop for about 2 to 3 days, stirring a few times daily.
7. When you are satisfied with the fermentation, add vanilla and some more water (to the preferred consistency) and stir until well combined. It should be slightly thicker than tomato sauce.
8. Cover and chill until use. Sprinkle cinnamon on top. Scatter roasted chickpeas on top and serve.

Probiotic Lemonade

Preparation Time: 15 Minutes | Cooking Time:0 | Servings: 4

Ingredients:

- Juice of 5 lemons or limes
- 1/2 cup whey
- 6 tablespoons sugar or sucanat
- 1/4 - 1 1/2 quarts filtered water

Directions:

1. Add sugar into the glass jar. Heat about 2 cups of the water and add into the jar. Stir until the sugar dissolves completely.
2. Add lemon juice and remaining water. Stir until well combined. Cool completely.
3. Add whey and stir.

4. Tighten the lid of the jar. Place the jar at room temperature for 2-3 days. Make sure that there is no sunlight falling on the jar.

5. Once it is fermented to your liking, place in the refrigerator until use.

Sima (Finnish Fermented Lemonade)

Preparation Time: 15 Minutes | Cooking Time: 8 – 10 hours | Servings: 7

Ingredients:

- organic lemon, thinly sliced
- 10 raisins
- 8 tablespoons + 2 teaspoons white sugar
- 8 tablespoons brown sugar
- 7 cups filtered water
- A large pinch yeast (less than 1/8 teaspoon)

Directions:

1. Boil water in a saucepan. Add brown sugar, 8 tablespoons white sugar Stir until the sugar dissolves completely.

2. Pour into the glass jar. Drop the lemon slices and cool until it is lukewarm

3. Partially cover the jar. Place the jar at room temperature 8 – 10 hours. Make sure that there is no sunlight falling on the jar.

4. Strain and divide the lemonade into the jars. Add a teaspoon of white sugar into each jar. Also add 5 raisins into each jar.

5. Tighten the cap of the bottles. Place the jar at room temperature for a couple of days or until the raisins will begin to float on top of the liquid. Stir a couple of times every day.

6. Chill until use. Open the cap briefly every other day to remove extra pressure from the bottles.

Sima with Fruits (Finnish Fizzy Fermented Fruit Coolers)

Preparation Time: 15 Minutes | Cooking Time: 6 – 12 hours | Servings: 6

Ingredients:

- gallon water
- 1 can (16 ounces) cranberry sauce
- 1 1/2 - 2 cups mulberries
- 1/3 cup pitted dates
- 1/2 pounds white sugar or more to taste
- 1 1/2 teaspoons ground ginger
- 1 1/4 pounds limes, thinly sliced
- 1/2 - 2/3 cup lemon juice
- 4 tablespoons raisins

To activate yeast:

- 1/4 cup water
- 5 – 8 raisins

Directions:

1. Add water, cranberry sauce, mulberries, dates, ground ginger, sugar, lime slices, lemon juice and raisins into a large pot.

2. Stir well and place the pot over high flame.

3. Let the mixture come to a boil. Stir often. Turn off the heat and pour into the brew bin.

4. Boil some more water (about 2 – 3 cups) and add into the bin. Keep the bin covered with a plastic sheet. Fasten with a rubber band. Set aside for a few hours until it cools completely.

5. To activate yeast: Add water and raisins into a small pot. Place the pot over medium flame. As the water begins to boil, turn off the heat.

6. Cover the pot with a fitting lid and set aside to cool completely.

7. Add the brewer's yeast and stir. Cover the pot once again and set aside for 6 – 12 hours.

8. Add activated yeast mixture into the bin and mix well. Bubbles should be visible and it should be foamy.

9. Keep the bin covered with a plastic sheet. Fasten with a rubber band. Place a sheet of

newspaper and place a small sheet of plywood over it.

10. Set aside in a cool and dry place for up to 3 weeks. The fermentation can take place in 2 days or it can take even 3 weeks.

11. When you are satisfied with the fermentation, pour into storage bottles. Tighten the caps and set aside on your countertop for a few more hours.

12. Chill and serve.

Wild Black Cherry Cordial

Preparation Time: 15 Minutes | Cooking Time:0 | Servings: 5

Ingredients:

- 2 1/2 cups ripe wild black cherries, discard stems, rinsed
- 2 1/2 cups organic cane sugar
- 7 1/2 cups cold water
- tablespoon citric acid or 4 tablespoons lemon juice

Directions:

1. Add cherries into the glass jar and mash the cherries using your hands.
2. Add sugar, water and citric acid and stir until sugar dissolves completely.
3. Cover the jar with cheesecloth. Do not cover the lid.
4. Place the jar in a cool and dry area.
5. Stir the mixture at the same time, every day. In a few days you will see bubbles in the mixture. Once you see the bubbles, taste a bit of the mixture every day. When you think it is the

taste you desire, it is time you store it. It should take 5 to 7 days in all.

6. Strain the mixture into a container and pour into jars. Label the jars with name and date.

7. Fasten the lids and refrigerate until use. It can last for about 3 months.

Sweet Potato Fly

Preparation Time: 5 Minutes | Cooking Time:0 | Servings: 4

Ingredients:

- large sweet potato, coarsely grated
- 1 cup sugar
- Juice of a lemon
- Zest of a lemon, grated
- Juice of a lemon
- 1/2 teaspoon ground nutmeg
- 1/2 egg shell, cleaned, crushed
- 1/2 gallon water
- 1/4 cup whey liquid
- 1 teaspoon ground cinnamon
- 1/4 teaspoon ground ginger

Directions:

1. Place the sweet potatoes in a sieve and rinse it under cold, running water.
2. Add sweet potatoes, sugar, lemon juice, lemon zest, water, whey, egg shell and spices into the brew bin and stir.
3. Close the lid and set aside at room temperature for 3 days or until you are satisfied with the fermentation.
4. Line the sieve with cheesecloth and strain the mixture into a pitcher.
5. Pour into storage bottles and refrigerate until use.

Lacto- Fermented Herbal Tea Drink

Preparation Time: 5 Minutes | Cooking Time: 10 Minutes | Servings: 4

Ingredients:

- 2 quarts fresh water
- 6 tablespoons honey or unrefined cane sugar
- 1/2 cup loose herbal tea of your choice
- 2/3 cup whey or kefir or 1/4 teaspoon powdered starter culture

Directions:

1. Pour water into a saucepan. Place the saucepan over high flame and let it come to a boil. Turn off the heat.
2. Place herbal tea in the saucepan and stir. Place a plate on the saucepan to cover it and let it sit for 10 minutes.
3. Strain the mixture into a pitcher and pour into the jar. Stir in honey and let it cool completely. Make sure that honey has dissolved completely.
4. Add whey and mix well using a wooden spoon. Cover the jar with cheesecloth and fasten it with a rubber band.
5. Keep the jar in a warm area for about 2 days. Make sure that there is no sunlight falling on the jar.
6. If you are not satisfied with the fermentation, add a little more honey or sugar and fasten the lid of the jar. Let it ferment for one more day.
7. It is ready to serve now. Serve at room temperature or chill and serve.

Ryazhenka, Russian Cultured Baked Milk

Preparation Time: 5 Minutes | Cooking Time: 6 – 8 hours | Servings: 1

Ingredients:

- quart fresh milk
- 1 tablespoon sour cream for every 2 cups of baked milk

Directions:

1. Pour milk into the slow cooker or Dutch oven.
2. If you are using the slow cooker, let the lid of the slow cooker be partially open. Set the slow cooker on low setting and timer for about 8 – 9 hours or until a golden crust is visible on top.
3. If you are using the Dutch oven, place a rack in the center of the oven and place the Dutch oven on the rack. Do not cover the pot.
4. Bake at 225 degree F for 6 – 8 hours or until a golden crust is visible on top.

5. Take out the golden crust and you can eat it. It is very tasty.
6. Place a strainer over a glass jar and strain the baked milk into it. Measure the baked milk and add sour cream accordingly.
7. Keep the jar covered with a tight fitting lid and place it on your countertop undisturbed until thick. It can take 4 – 12 hours.
8. Chill until use. It can last for 2 – 3 weeks. You can eat it with a spoon, as it will be very thick. If you want to drink it, spoon it into a shaker and shake it vigorously for about a minute. Pour into a glass and serve.

Makgeolli (Korean Rice Liquor)

Preparation Time: 5 Minutes | Cooking Time: 3 hours 15 Minutes | Servings: 8

Ingredients:

- 2 1/2 cups short grain rice, rinsed, soaked in water for 2 – 3 hours, drained
- 1/2 package dry yeast
- 2 tablespoons sugar (optional)
- 3/4 cup nuruk (starter culture)
- 10 – 12 cups water

Directions:

1. Add rice and 4 cups of water into the pot. Place the pot over medium-high flame.
2. Cover the pot and cook for 15 minutes. Mix up the rice using a wooden spoon.
3. Cover the pot once again and cook on low for 15 minutes.
4. Turn off the heat and add the rice into the electric dehydrator's baskets.

5. Cover the dehydrator and dry for 3 hours at 160 degree F. The rice grain should be hard outside. In case you do not have a dehydrator, place the rice in baskets and dry it in the sun where there is lots of breeze.

6. Transfer the rice into the earthenware crock along with 4 cups of water and nuruk yeast and stir well using a wooden spoon.

7. Place cotton cloth on top of the crock and close the lid. Set aside for 10 – 15 hours.

8. Stir once again and cover the pot back, along with the cloth. Set aside on your countertop all night.

9. Stir once again in the morning with the wooden spoon. The mixture will be having more liquid than the previous day. Set it aside for 4 – 5 days, making sure to stir 3 – 4 times daily. As the days go by, the mixture will be thinner than the previous day.

10. Place the nylon bag in a pitcher. Add the fermented rice into the bag and squeeze the bag to remove as much liquid as possible.

11. Pour into bottles. Place the bottles in the refrigerator for a couple of days.

12. Serve chilled. It can last for 2 – 3 weeks.

Chapter 11: Deydrated Recipes

Carrot Pulp Crackers

Preparation Time: 5 Minutes | Cooking Time: 18 hours and 30 minutes | Servings: 12

Ingredients:

- 2 cups carrot pulp
- cup almonds, soaked in water overnight, nicely rinsed and drained
- 1 tablespoon dried onion
- 1 tablespoon ground chia seeds
- cups water
- 1/2 teaspoon red pepper flakes
- 1/2 teaspoon smoked paprika
- 1 tablespoon coconut aminos
- tablespoons ground flax seed
- 1 teaspoon Italian seasoning

Directions:

1. Add the almonds to a food processor.
2. Process until crumbly.
3. Stir in the rest of the rest of the ingredients.
4. Pulse until fully combined.
5. Spread the mixture on the dehydrator tray.
6. Dehydrate at 125 degrees F for 2 hours.
7. Score the crackers.
8. Reduce temperature to 115 degrees F.
9. Dehydrate for 8 hours.
10. Flip and dehydrate for another 8 hours.
11. Store the carrot crackers in a container with lid for up to 7 days.

Green Crackers

Preparation Time: 15 Minutes | Cooking Time: 8 hours and 30 minutes | Servings: 6

Ingredients:

- cup green juice pulp
- 1/4 cup nutritional yeast
- 1/4 cup chia seeds
- 1/4 cup ground flax seeds
- 1 tablespoon tamari
- tablespoons sesame seeds
- 1/2 teaspoon salt
- 1/4 cup water

Directions:

1. Combine the green juice pulp, nutritional yeast, chia seeds, ground flax seeds, tamari, sesame seeds, salt and water in your food processor.
2. Pulse until fully combined.
3. Gradually spread a layer of the mixture on the dehydrator tray.
4. Score the mixture into crackers.
5. Dehydrate at 115 degrees F for 5 hours.
6. Flip and dehydrate for another 3 hours.
7. Store the crackers in an airtight container for up to 4 days or freeze for up to 1 month.

Seaweed Crackers

Preparation Time: 25 Minutes | Cooking Time: 25 hours and 10 minutes | Servings: 4

Ingredients:

- cup flax seeds
- 1 1/2 cups water
- tablespoons tamari
- 1/2 cup nori sheets, torn into smaller pieces

Directions:

1. Soak the flaxseeds in the water for 1 hour.
2. Stir in the tamari and nori sheets.
3. Place a tablespoonful of the mixture on the dehydrator tray.
4. Dehydrate at 110 degrees F for 14 hours.
5. Flip and dehydrate for another 10 hours.

Onion & Nut Crackers

Preparation Time: 30 Minutes | Cooking Time: 2 hours and 20 minutes | Servings: 12

Ingredients:

- green onion stalk
- 1 garlic clove
- 1 cup cashews
- 1 cup sunflower seeds
- 1/4 cup coconut aminos
- 1/2 cup water

Directions:

1. Add the green onion, garlic, cashews, sunflower seeds, coconut aminos and water to your blender or food processor.
2. Cover your dehydrator tray with parchment paper.
3. Gradually spread a thin layer of the mixture on the tray.
4. Dehydrate at 115 degrees F for 1 hour.
5. Reduce temperature to 105 degrees F.
6. Score the crackers.
7. Dehydrate for another 1 hour.
8. Store the crackers in an airtight container.

Graham, Peanut Butter & Banana Crackers

Preparation Time: 35 Minutes | Cooking Time: 12 hours and 30 minutes | Servings: 8

Ingredients:
- 3 ripe bananas, sliced
- 1/2 cup peanut butter
- 3 cups crushed graham crackers

- cup ground peanuts
- 1/2 teaspoon cinnamon powder

Directions:

1. Mash the bananas using a fork.
2. Stir in the peanut butter.
3. Add the rest of the ingredients.
4. Mix well.
5. Make a ball from the mixture.
6. Roll out the mixture onto a baking sheet lined with parchment paper.
7. Cover and refrigerate for 6 hours.
8. Score the crackers.
9. Transfer to the dehydrator tray.
10. Dehydrate at 145 degrees F for 6 hours.

Coconut Cookies

Preparation Time: 25 Minutes | Cooking Time: 6 hours and 20 minutes | Servings: 6

Ingredients:

- cup peanut butter
- 1 cup dried apricots
- 1 cup coconut flakes
- cups dates, pitted
- 1/4 cup water

Directions:

1. First, add all the ingredients to your food processor.
2. Pulse until fully combined.

3. Form balls from the mixture.
4. Next, press the balls to form cookies.
5. Place the cookies on the dehydrator tray.
6. Dehydrate at 175 degrees F for 6hours.

Oatmeal Cashew Cookies

Preparation Time: 25 Minutes | Cooking Time: 12 hours and 30 minutes | Servings: 4

Ingredients:

- 2 cups oats
- 1/2 cup cashews
- 1/2 cup almonds, chopped
- 3/4 cup dates
- 1/2 cup raisins, chopped
- 2 apples, grated
- 3 teaspoons pumpkin spice

Directions:

1. Add the oats to your food processor.
2. Grind until powdered.
3. Transfer to a bowl.
4. Grind the cashews and almonds until consistency is similar to flour.
5. Stir into the oats.
6. Add the rest of the ingredients.
7. Mix well.
8. Form cookies from the mixture.
9. Dehydrate at 90 degrees F for 12 hours.

Kiwi Chips

Preparation Time: 5 Minutes | Cooking Time: 12 hours and 10 minutes | Servings: 6

Ingredients:

- 4 kiwis, peeled and sliced

Directions:

1. Arrange the kiwi slices on the dehydrator tray.
2. Dehydrate at 135 degrees F for 12 hours, checking every 4 hours.
3. Store in your airtight container for up to 5 days.

Strawberry Yogurt Drops

Preparation Time: 5 Minutes | Cooking Time: *8* hours and 20 minutes | Servings: 10

Ingredients:

- 3/4 cup strawberry flavored yogurt
- egg white

Directions:

1. Beat the egg white until you see stiff peaks forming.
2. Stir in the yogurt and mix well.
3. Line your dehydrator tray with parchment paper.
4. Place the mixture inside a piping bag.
5. Squeeze the piping bag to make small drops on the dehydrator tray.
6. Add the yogurt drops to the dehydrator tray.
7. Dehydrate at 120 degrees F for 8 hours.

Pear Chips

Preparation Time: 5 Minutes | Cooking Time: 12 hours and 20 minutes | Servings: 10

Ingredients:

- 10 pears, sliced thinly
- cup lemon juice

Directions:

1. Dip each of the pear slices in the lemon juice.
2. Next, arrange the pear slices in a single layer on the dehydrator tray.
3. Then, dehydrate at 130 degrees F for 12 hours.
4. Store in an airtight container.

3-Ingredient Banana Raisin Cookies

Preparation Time: 5 Minutes | Cooking Time: 6-8 hours | Servings: 2

Ingredients:

- very ripe banana, mashed
- 1 cup raisins
- 1 cup sweetened flake coconut

Directions:

1. Rehydrate raisins for 20 minutes in warm water.
2. Combine banana, raisins and coconut in a food processor until a paste forms.
3. Dehydrate for 6-8 hours at 110 degrees. Flip mixture over and dehydrate for another 6 hours.

Apple Pie Leather

Preparation Time: 5 Minutes | Cooking Time: 8-24 hours | Servings: 4

Ingredients:

- 6 apples, peeled, cored and chopped

- cup coconut milk
- cups applesauce
- 1/4 cup honey
- 1 tsp. ground cinnamon
- 1 tsp. apple pie spice
- Tbsp. finely chopped raisins

Directions:

1. Place all ingredients in a food processor and pulse once or twice.
2. Spread mixture on greased fruit leather dehydrator sheets.
3. Dehydrate for 8-24 hours at 135 degrees.
4. Cut into strips and roll into cylinders.

Asian Pear and Ginger Treats

Preparation Time: 5 Minutes | Cooking Time: 9-12 hours | Servings: 4

Ingredients:

- 6 medium sized Asian pears, peeled, pitted and cored
- 1/2 tsp. honey
- 4 Tbsp. warm water
- 1 small knob of ginger, finely grated

Directions:

1. In a bowl, mix honey and ginger. Add the water and mix well.
2. Slice Asian pears into uniform slices, around 1/4 inch thick. Arrange pear slices onto dehydrator tray and brush with a thin layer of ginger-honey mixture.
3. Dehydrate for 9-12 hours at 135 degrees.

Banana Cocoa Leather

Preparation Time: 10 Minutes | Cooking Time: 8-10 hours | Servings: 2

Ingredients:

- 4 bananas
- 2 Tbsp. cocoa powder
- 1-2 Tbsp. corn syrup
- tsp. lemon juice

Directions:

1. Puree all ingredients until smooth.
2. Pour mixture onto dehydrator trays and spread to 1/4 inch thickness. Dehydrate at 130 degree for 8-10 hours. About half way through, flip leather to the other side.

Cherry Coconut Almond Cookies

Preparation Time: 10 Minutes | Cooking Time: 6 hours | Servings: 2

Ingredients:

- cup salted almond butter
- 1 cup pitted dates (soaked in water for 1/2 hour)
- 1 cup dried cherries (soaked in water for 1/2 hour)
- 1 cup crushed almonds
- 1/8- 1/4 cup water
- 1 cup shredded coconut

Directions:

1. In a food processor, pulse the dried fruits. Add almond butter and crushed almonds. Pulse again.

2. Add in water slowly until the dough is able to be rolled into balls. Do not allow dough to get too runny. Flatten balls into discs and dip into shredded coconut to adhere to both sides.
3. Place on dehydrator sheet and set temperature to 145 degrees. Dehydrate for 3 hours and then flip over to other side for 3 hours.

Chewy Lemony Treats

Preparation Time: 10 Minutes | Cooking Time: 8 hours | Servings: 2

Ingredients:

- 2 cups almonds
- 2 cups unsweetened coconut flakes
- 6 Tbsp. lemon juice
- tsp. vanilla extract
- Dash of cinnamon
- 1/4 cup maple syrup

Directions:

1. Place almonds in the food processor and pulse until a flour-like consistency develops.
2. Add coconut and process with the ground nuts. Add the lemon juice, (zest if using), vanilla extract, cinnamon and maple syrup.
3. Scoop out batter into mini-balls and flatten. Place on dehydrator sheets and dehydrate for 8 hours at 115 degrees for a chewy texture.

Energy Balls

Preparation Time: 10 Minutes | Cooking Time: 3 hours | Servings: 3

Ingredients:

- 1/2 cup raw cashews, soaked
- cups dates, soaked
- 1/2 cup raisins
- 5 Tbsp. unsweetened cocoa powder
- Tbsp. maple syrup
- 1/2 tsp. vanilla extract
- 1/2 tsp. salt
- 1/2 cup crushed cashews
- 1/2 cup unsweetened coconut flakes

Directions:

1. Remove cashews and dates from soaking water. Place them in a food processor and pulse. Add the raisins, cocoa powder, maple syrup, vanilla extract and salt and blend until it reaches a paste-like consistency.
2. Once the mixture feels like a dough, roll into balls. Mix crushed cashews and coconut flakes in a small bowl and roll the balls in the mixture.
3. Place balls on dehydrator trays and dry at 135 degrees for 3 hours.

Fruit Sprinkles

Preparation Time: 10 Minutes | Cooking Time: 6-8 hours | Servings: 2

Ingredients:

- cup raspberries or strawberries, hulled
- 1 Tbsp. sugar
- 1 Tbsp. orange juice
- Zest of 2 lemons
- Zest of 2 oranges

Directions:

1. Dice strawberries and raspberries into small pieces.
2. Combine with sugar, juice and lemon and orange zest.
3. Spread mixture on dehydrator sheets.
4. Dehydrate for 6-8 hours at 118 degrees. At this point, fruit should be completely dried.
5. Place mixture in a spice grinder and pulse several times until you have sprinkles. Top

your favorite treats with fruit sprinkles for added flavor and color.

Goji Berry Leather

Preparation Time: 10 Minutes | Cooking Time: 6-7 hours | Servings: 2

Ingredients:

- cup dried goji berries
- cups unsweetened applesauce
- Tbsp. honey

Directions:

1. Place goji berries in 1 cup of water and let soak until they are rehydrated, about 1 hour.
2. Pour berries, soaking water, applesauce and honey into the blender and blend until smooth. Add more water if necessary.
3. Spread onto dehydrator sheets and dry at 135 degrees for 6-7 hours.

Honey Banana Walnut Chips

Preparation Time: 10 Minutes | Cooking Time: 6-12 hours | Servings: 2

Ingredients:

- 4 bananas, peeled and cut into 1/4 pieces
- 1/4 cup honey, diluted slightly with water
- 1/2 cup crushed walnuts

Directions:

1. Dip banana slices into diluted honey. Sprinkle with crushed walnuts.
2. Place bananas on dehydrator trays and dry at 135 degrees for 2 hours. Then set the temperature at 115 degrees and dehydrate for another 6-12 hours.

Nothing But Fruit Bars

Preparation Time: 10 Minutes | Cooking Time: 18 hours | Servings: 2

Ingredients:

- 2 cups sprouted buckwheat or quinoa
- cup dates
- 1 cup dried apricots
- 1 Tbsp. cinnamon
- 1/8 tsp. cardamom
- 1 pear or apple, peeled, cored and diced

Directions:

1. Place all ingredients in a blender. Blend until smooth.
2. Spread the mixture onto dehydrator trays. Use a spatula to smooth. Dehydrate for 18 hours at 130 degrees.

Raspberry Banana Fruit Leather

Preparation Time: 10 Minutes | Cooking Time: 8-10 hours | Servings: 2

Ingredients:

- banana
- 1 cup raspberries
- Tbsp. raspberry jam
- 1 tsp. lemon juice

Directions:

1. Puree banana, raspberries, jam and lemon juice until smooth.
2. Spread mixture evenly, about 1/8 inch thick, onto fruit leather sheets.
3. Set the temperature to 135 degrees. Dry for 8-10 hours, or until leathery to touch.

4. Raw Fig Balls

Preparation Time: 10 Minutes | Cooking Time: 4-6 hours | Servings: 2

Ingredients:

- cup raw almonds
- 10 dried figs
- 1/2 cup raisins
- 1/2 tsp. almond extract
- 1/2 tsp. vanilla extract
- 3/4 cup unsweetened coconut flakes

Directions:

1. Place the almonds in a food processor and pulse until they are ground. Add the figs, raisins and extracts and pulse until well combined.
2. Once the mixture is a dough-like consistency, roll into balls. Roll the balls in the coconut flakes.
3. Place balls on dehydrator trays and dry at 135 degrees for 4-6 hours.

Spicy Strawberry Fruit Leather

Preparation Time: 15 Minutes | Cooking Time: 6-8 hours | Servings: 1

Ingredients:

- lb strawberries, hulled and chopped
- 1/3 cup granulated sugar
- 1 Tbsp. lemon juice
- 1 jalapeno or serrano pepper, seeds removed

Directions:

1. Puree strawberries, sugar, lemon juice and pepper.
2. Pour mixture onto fruit leather sheet of your dehydrator. Spread puree evenly, about 1/8 inch thick, onto drying tray.
3. Set the temperature to 140 degrees. Dry for 6-8 hours, or touch center of leather to determine dryness.

Sweet and Sour Cranberries

Preparation Time: 15 Minutes | Cooking Time: 12-16 hours | Servings: 2

Ingredients:

- 12 oz. cranberries
- 1/4 cup corn syrup (or sugar)
- Zest of one orange and one lime

Directions:

1. Place cranberries in a bowl and pour boiling water over them until the skins crack. Drain.
2. Toss the berries with corn syrup or sugar and zests. Place berries on cooking sheet and freeze for 2 hours to promote faster drying.
3. Assemble berries on a mesh sheet in the dehydrator and dry at 135 degrees for 12-16 hours or until chewy.

Sweet "Caramel Apples

Preparation Time: 5 Minutes | Cooking Time: 10-12 hours | Servings: 2

Ingredients:

- 3-4 Granny Smith apples
- 1/2 cup store-bought caramel sauce

Directions:

1. Slice the apple into thin rounds, between 1/8-1/4 inch thick. Peels can be removed or left intact. Remove core and seeds.
2. Use a pastry brush to spread a small amount of caramel onto each apple round.
3. Arrange in a single line in your dehydrator and set temperature to 135 degrees. Allow apples to dehydrate for 10-12 hours.

Tangy Dried Mangos

Preparation Time: 5 Minutes | Cooking Time: 8-9 hours | Servings: 2

Ingredients:

- 4-5 ripe mangoes
- Tbsp. honey
- 1/4 cup lime juice
- Pinch of salt

Directions:

1. Peel and slice mangoes into thin, even strips.
2. Dissolve honey in lemon juice. Mix well and add salt.
3. Dip mango slices into honey mixture. Shake off excess.
4. Arrange in a single line in your dehydrator and set temperature to 135 degrees. Allow mangoes to dehydrate for 8-9 hours.

Tropical Pineapple Crisps

Preparation Time: 15 Minutes | Cooking Time: 12-16 hours | Servings: 2

Ingredients:

- ripe pineapple
- 1 cup Coconut oil
- 1/2 cup sweetened coconut flakes
- Sea salt to taste

Directions:

1. Peel and core the pineapple. Slice into thin, uniform rounds about 1/2 inch thick.
2. Using a pastry brush, spread a thin layer of coconut oil on each pineapple slice. Sprinkle with coconut flakes and a small amount of sea salt.
3. Arrange in a single line in your dehydrator and set temperature to 135 degrees. Allow pineapple to dehydrate for 12-16 hours, flipping the slices halfway through for even dryness.

Chapter 12: Measurement Conversion Tables

Volume Equivalents (Liquid)

US STANDARD	US STANDARD (OUNCES)	METRIC (APPROXIMATE)
2 tablespoons	1 fl. oz.	30 mL
1/4 cup	2 fl. oz.	60 mL
1/2 cup	4 fl. oz.	120 mL
1 cup	8 fl. oz.	240 mL
1-1/2 cups	12 fl. oz.	355 mL
2 cups or 1 pint	16 fl. oz.	475 mL
4 cups or 1 quart	32 fl. oz.	1 L
1 gallon	128 fl. oz.	4 L

Volume Equivalents (Dry)

US STANDARD	METRIC (APPROXIMATE)
1/8 teaspoon	0.5 mL
1/4 teaspoon	1 mL
1/2 teaspoon	2 mL
3/4 teaspoon	4 mL
1 teaspoon	5 mL
1 tablespoon	15 mL
1/4 cup	59 mL

1/3 cup	79 mL
1/2 cup	118 mL
2/3 cup	156 mL
3/4 cup	177 mL
1 cup	235 mL
2 cups or 1 pint	475 mL
3 cups	700 mL
4 cups or 1 quart	1 L

Oven Temperatures

FAHRENHEIT (F)	CELSIUS (C) (APPROXIMATE)
250°	120°
300°	150°
325°	165°
350°	180°
375°	190°
400°	200°
425°	220°
450°	230°

Review this Book

Hey!

Thanks for reading my cookbook. If you found this helpful book or found exciting insights into your passion, I invite you to leave a positive review for this book.

It costs you nothing, and as far as I'm concerned, you could help spread my work to so many more people.

I'm sure you will now perfectly master the art of preserving your favorite foods.

Here's how to do it:

You can frame with your phone's camera this QR code

Or alternatively, you can directly paste this link into your favorite browser.

https://amz.run/5KY2

Thanks for your feedback and your excellent availability.

Conclusion

Thank you for reading this book. Whether you are a gardener, a cook, or a homesteader, you have probably learned or will learn how to preserve food through canning. These small nuggets of information will help you when home canning foods.

You can be part of the modern revival of canning, something your grandmother probably did. Canning and preserving produce high-quality, flavorful foods that save you money.

Canning has the potential to be a great solution for many people who are trying to find a cheaper and healthier way to eat, store, and preserve their foods. After the initial investment that comes in the form of buying canning supplies, canning your own food in the comfort of your kitchen can be a rewarding – and economic – experience. For beginners who are just trying to figure out whether they'd like to take canning up as for the long-term, you do not have to go all out and buy all the supplies. There are many alternatives to the standard canning supplies that you can purchase – they tend to be cheaper and just as effective as the original canning supplies.

Canning offers you the opportunity to preserve several foods from the comfort of your own home!

You do need to know, though, that there are different methods for different foods. Some methods involve boiling water; other methods involve pressure cookers and other tools. With every method, there are different sets of supplies needed. If you are a beginner, you will struggle with finding the appropriate tools and selecting the right methods for canning and preserving your foods.

Good luck.